A Spacious
Heart

Christian Mission and Modern Culture

EDITED BY
ALAN NEELY, H. WAYNE PIPKIN,
AND WILBERT R. SHENK

In the series:

A Spacious Heart

Essays on Identity and Belonging

JUDITH M. GUNDRY-VOLF

MIROSLAV VOLF

TRINITY PRESS INTERNATIONAL
Harrisburg, Pennsylvania

Gracewing.

First published by
Trinity Press International
P.O. Box 1321
Harrisburg, PA 17105
U.S.A.

First British edition
Gracewing
2 Southern Avenue
Leominster
Herefordshire HR6 0QF
England

Trinity Press International is part of the Morehouse Group.

Library of Congress Cataloging-in-Publication Data
Gundry-Volf, Judith M.
    A spacious heart : essays on identity and belonging / Judith
M. Gundry-Volf, Miroslav Volf.
        p.   cm. − (Christian mission and modern culture)
    Includes bibliographical references.
    ISBN 1-56338-201-6 (pbk. : alk. paper)
    1. Multiculturalism − Religious aspects − Christianity.   2.
Jesus Christ − Political and social views.   3. Syrophoenician woman
(Biblical figure).   4. Samaritan woman (Biblical figure).   5. Bosnia
and Hercegovina − Ethnic relations.   6. Yugoslav War, 1991- −
Atrocities.   I. Volf, Miroslav.   II. Title.   III. Series.
BR115.C8G795   1997
261−dc20   97−12709
                                                                   CIP

Gracewing ISBN 0-85244-465-6

Printed in the United States of America

97   98   99   00   01   02   6   5   4   3   2   1

Contents

93060

Preface to the Series

Both Christian mission and modern culture, widely regarded as antagonists, are in crisis. The emergence of the modern mission movement in the early nineteenth century cannot be understood apart from the rise of technocratic society. Now, at the end of the twentieth century, both modern culture and Christian mission face an uncertain future.

One of the developments integral to modernity was the way the role of religion in culture was redefined. Whereas religion had played an authoritative role in the culture of Christendom, modern culture was highly critical of religion and increasingly secular in its assumptions. A sustained effort was made to banish religion to the backwaters of modern culture.

The decade of the 1980s witnessed further momentous developments on the geopolitical front with the collapse of communism. In the aftermath of the breakup of the system of power blocs that dominated international relations for a generation, it is clear that religion has survived even if its institutionalization has undergone deep change and its future forms are unclear. Secularism continues to oppose religion, while technology has emerged as a major source of power and authority in modern culture. Both confront Christian faith with fundamental questions.

The purpose of this series is to probe these developments from a variety of angles with a view to helping the church understand its missional responsibility to a culture in crisis. One important resource is the church's experience of two centuries of cross-cultural mission that has reshaped the church into a global Christian *ecumene*. The focus of our inquiry will be the church in modern culture. The series (1) examines modern/postmodern culture from a missional point of view; (2) develops the theological agenda that the church in modern culture must address in order to recover its own integrity; and (3) tests fresh conceptualizations of the nature and mission of the church as it engages modern culture. In other words, these volumes are intended to be a forum where conventional assumptions can be challenged and alternative formulations explored.

This series is a project authorized by the Institute of Mennonite Studies, research agency of the Associated Mennonite Biblical Seminary, and supported by a generous grant from the Pew Charitable Trusts.

Editorial Committee

ALAN NEELY
H. WAYNE PIPKIN
WILBERT R. SHENK

Introduction

Miroslav Volf

A Perfect Hell on Earth

"There are no devils left in hell," the missionary said. "They are all in Rwanda." Rwanda — where people were hunted down on the streets like animals and killed where they were caught; where blood flowed down the aisles of churches made into the preferred places of massacre by a perverse inversion of symbolism; where butchered bodies floated down the river — on their way to Ethiopia, via the shortcut of the Nayaborongo River, where the hated Tutsi "intruders" came from. "The fighting was hand to hand," writes a reporter, "intimate and unspeakable, a kind of bloodlust that left those who managed to escape it hollow-eyed and mute" (Gibbs 1994:58). In only three months a million were dead and more than twice as many driven out of their homes. The protagonists of the genocide were for the most part Christians!

In a sense, it would be less disturbing had the Rwandan genocide just erupted out of the atavistic depths of its protagonists' souls. But it did not. It was carefully orchestrated — a well-planned attempt at a "final solution" (see Block 1994:3–8). If one asks what caused it, one gets the same answer as in the case of so many other ethnic

1

wars. Alex de Waal writes: "The elements of the story can be sought in desperate land pressure in Rwanda, in rural poverty intensified by the collapse of international coffee prices, and in the determination of a privileged coterie to retain their commanding positions in the Government and the army in the face of political and economic 'readjustment' of the state. These have been fuel for the fire. But what ignited the genocide is an extremist racial ideology, an ideology that would be laughable were it not so demonically powerful" (1994:l). Mix economic deprivation and lust for power, add to it racist ideology and let it simmer for a while, and you will get Rwanda of 1994 — a perfect hell on earth.

"There are no devils left in hell; they are all in Rwanda." The words seem to paint just the right image to express the unfathomable. Yet if we leave the immediacy of the Rwandan brutalities and consider the larger world, we sense that the image is skewed on two important counts. First, *all* devils are not in Rwanda. If the missionary's words were not a cry of desperation, one might even be able to detect in them a tinge of clandestine racism: a little country in black Africa has sucked up all the black devils. But what about Bosnia? What about Nagorno-Karabakh? What about the fifty or so other spots around the globe — Western countries included — where violence has erupted among people who share the same terrain but differ in ethnicity, race, language, or religion? No devils there? Without intending to diminish the horror of Rwanda's genocide, we must say that the devils of vicious ethnic strife are by no means all *there*. They are dispersed around the globe, sowing death and desolation, even if less vehemently than did the devils of Rwanda.

The second way in which the missionary's comment on

Rwanda is skewed is even more disturbing than the first. The global presence of devils notwithstanding, hell has by no means become an empty place. In the dark kingdom of evil potencies, fresh troops are being trained for new assignments. The signs of the coming woes are evident in disturbing developments of global proportions. Rapid population growth, diminishing resources, unemployment, migration to shantytowns, and lack of education are steadily increasing pressure along the many social fault lines of our globe. Though we cannot predict exactly when and where the social quakes will occur and what their magnitude will be, we can be sure that the earth will shake (see Kennedy 1994).

As the image of fault lines suggests, clashes will take place along the boundary lines of social groups. Today, after the breakdown of a bipolar world, social tectonic plates are defined less by ideology than by culture. As Samuel Huntington (1993:22) argues, on a global scale the fault lines between major civilizations — the broadest level of cultural identity people have — "will be the battle lines of the future." Similarly, within civilizations, the coming wars will be fought between discrete cultural and ethnic groups. The conditions seem ripe for more Rwandas and Bosnias in the future. The kingdom of darkness has not exhausted its resources. There are plenty more devils in hell ready to make more hells on earth.

The Politics of Difference

Rwanda is far away, tucked in the heart of Africa; Rwanda is tribal, untouched by the 'blessings' of modernization. The West, someone might argue, can grieve for Rwanda's dead and help Rwanda's living, but Rwanda's problems are not Western problems.

In response, we might point to the flames that in 1992 engulfed Los Angeles as African-Americans, Korean Americans, Hispanics, and Whites clashed. Or we could draw your attention to Nazi skinheads in Germany who do not shy away from violence as they fight, in the name of a mono-ethnic *Volk*, the arrival of a multicultural society in Germany. Instead, let us go briefly to the Canadian province of Quebec, to urban Montreal, to Claude Béland, a man whose finger is on forty billion dollars worth of investment funds. In Béland's Quebec, French nationalism is thriving, and secessionist impulses remain strong. Here we find some of the same search for communal identity coupled with desire for economic power that we encounter on the streets of Berlin or Los Angeles.

As Michael Ignatieff's conversation with the Montreal bank president, in his book *Blood and Belonging*, reveals:

Claude Béland looks like a North American bank president: silver-haired, immaculately suited in sober blue, with a fluent English that he uses to take calls from fellow bank presidents in Chicago, New York, Los Angeles, and London. Yet what other major North American bank president's native tongue is French? What other North American bank president is a nationalist?

He wasn't to begin with. Like the cautious accountant that he is, he thought sovereignty [that of Quebec] was too risky an option in the 1970s and early 1980s. Now he has changed his mind. Why?

"Well, because a state is the only way to protect the identity of a people, you know. Identity I define as the harmony between your values and your actions. In other words, you know who you are and you want to protect that... and be recognized for that."

It seems odd to me, [continues Ignatieff,] that a bank president should be talking about such metaphysical entities as identity, so I ask him whether statehood matters because it confers identity or because it completes an economic emancipation. Which is it, the pocketbook or the soul? Béland doesn't want to have to choose. Independence, he says, is about both dimensions (1993: 151).

The search for communal identity our bank president is musing about — Quebecois nationalism — has in the past often been associated with a revolt against modernity, with a nostalgic reaction of disenfranchised peoples. As Ignatieff (:154) points out, nationalism functioned as "a defense of the backwardness of economically beleaguered or declining classes and regions from the flames of individualism, capitalism, Judaism, and so on." Not so in Quebec. Nationalism here is no longer a "nationalism of resentment," "a vocabulary of regret for what modernity has done to the distinctiveness of Quebec society" (:162, 154). The old scores have been settled, and the Quebecois have embraced modernity. Nationalism now functions as "a rhetoric of self-affirmation" (:162).

The key words in the previous paragraphs are "identity," "recognition," "self-affirmation." They connect what is happening in Rwanda, on the streets of Los Angeles, and in Quebec. Charles Taylor (1992:38) can help us understand the significance of these concepts. In his book *Multiculturalism and the Politics of Recognition*, he distinguishes between the "politics of equal dignity" and the "politics of difference." The politics of equal dignity seek to establish what is universally the same, "an identical basket of rights and immunities." Sometimes the politics of equal dignity or equal worth is combined with what one might call the "politics of equal wealth." In addition to establishing an identical basket of rights and immunities, people seek to establish an identical basket of goods and services. As the word *equal* makes plain — *equal* worth, *equal* wealth — in both cases you are dealing with something universal.

Not so in the case of the politics of difference. "With the politics of difference," writes Taylor: "What we are asked to recognize is the unique identity of this individual or group, their distinctiveness from everyone else. The idea is that it is precisely this distinctness that has been ignored, glossed over, assimilated to a dominant or majority identity. And this assimilation is the cardinal sin against the ideal of authenticity" (:38).

Faced with assimilating tendencies, various groups in the West are struggling today for recognition of their distinct identity: as women, African-Americans, Hispanics, and so forth. What informs the struggle is the belief that "nonrecognition or misrecognition can inflict harm, can be a form of oppression, imprisoning someone in a false, distorted, and reduced mode of being" (Taylor 1992:25). The need for recognition of a specific identity can be combined with the requirement of a "specific system of group-conscious policies and rights" in addition to "a general system of rights which are the same for all" (see Young 1990:174).

Much of the debate about multiculturalism in Western societies today has to do with the struggle for recognition of the cultures of discrete groups within our societies. Contrast the multiculturalism of the 1990s with the American liberation movements of the 1960s. Louis Menand writes: "The civil rights movement, the women's movement, and the gay liberation movement were about equity: they based their moral appeal on the principles of liberty and equality that democracies are committed to uphold — the right to vote, to have equal access to educational and economic opportunity, to live where one chooses, and so forth" (1994:18).

In contrast to such liberation movements, multiculturalism is not about equity. Multiculturalism "is about culture. *Its* moral appeal is based on the feeling of many women and gay and non-white Americans that although legal barriers to equality may have been largely removed, cultural barriers remain.... [M]any people in these non-traditional groups felt that the old ways *were* racially and sexually self-serving — or, at a minimum, were oblivious of the interests and perspectives other people might have — and that they amounted to a subtle form of exclusion which antidiscrimination policies of the civil rights type could do very little to remedy" (Menand 1994:18). The struggle for the equality of individuals belonging to various social groups has given way to the struggle for recognition of communal identities.

So far we have underlined the importance of group identities within non-Western societies (such as the struggle between Hutus and Tutsi) and within Western societies (such as the struggle for Quebecois identity or debates over multiculturalism). In addition to the struggle between various cultural, ethnic, and religious groups *within* Western societies, however, there are serious tensions emerging *between* Western and non-Western cultures. In the report of the UNESCO International Expert Group entitled *The Multicultural Planet* we read: "The majority of today's cultures, fearing degenerative change, resist further influences from more powerful cultures; with few exceptions, the non-western cultures are on the defensive. . . . [For instance] Latin Americans are aware that they are passive receivers rather than active producers of the cultural currents that shape the contemporary world; they feel dependent on the outside world and in particular on the United States" (1993:87). Will the global exchange of ideas, goods, and services lead to the formation of a single homogenous global culture shaped largely by Western values, or will indigenous cultures be powerful enough to preserve their own vitality? In many regions "a new brand of cultural nationalism is emerging in reaction against deepening dependency and subordination" (:187). We can expect a clash between indigenous cultures and the global technological monoculture.

Cultural Identity as a Theological Task

The emergence of the politics of difference in Western societies, the resurgence of ethnic and cultural conflicts in the non-Western world, and the clash between modern technological and traditional cultures on the global plane suggest that cultural differences will be an important bone of contention in the future. These social developments confront Christian theology with new challenges. In recent decades, theologians have poured much energy into thinking about human rights and economic justice. It was assumed that the problems associated with *group identities* would take care of themselves, an expectation shared by both liberal and socialist political philosophy. But they did not. If we continue to treat group identities as neglected orphans, we should not be surprised if they behave as unruly children. It is high time to give them serious and sustained attention.

Christian theology has significant resources for reflecting on the relations between cultures. For example, from its very inception the church was a multicultural community. Consider the Day of Pentecost, the birthday of the church. Jews from "every nation under heaven" hear the disciples speaking in their own native language (Acts 2:3–7); they believe and are joined in one community of faith. When the Spirit comes, all understand each other, and yet each hears (and speaks) his or her own language. Pentecost, as the beginning of the new age of God's salvation, is not a reversion to the unity of cultural uniformity; it is an advance toward harmony in cultural diversity. Similarly, in Ephesians the church owes its very being to the fact that Christ has brought near those who were "far off" by making both groups "one" and "has broken down the dividing wall of hostility" between them (Eph. 2:13–14). Whether "Jew" or "Greek," Christians found themselves reconciled in one community of faith.

Drawing on the resources from their own rich tradition, the Christian churches should be at the forefront of the struggle for a just peace between cultures. Often, however, they seem helpless in the face of the sinister powers that stir hatreds between cultures and animate destructive urges. Sometimes they even find themselves accomplices of the evil that they have either been too blind to perceive or too impotent to resist. Occasionally they can be found among the worst perpetrators.

The two essays contained in this book are an attempt to explore some key aspects of the problem of diverse group identities. They offer some preliminary exegetical and theological perspectives on the encounter with "others." The essays arose out of shared experience, move toward the same goal, and take parallel routes to get there.

The essays are shaped by three contexts, which in turn have shaped us both individually and together. One is that of urban violence between various ethnic and cultural groups in the multicultural city of Los Angeles where we presently live; we wrote the essays while the fires that engulfed Los Angeles in 1992 were still smoldering. The second context is the war between Croatians, Muslims, and Serbs in former Yugoslavia where we lived and worked for a number of years and where we still regularly teach. The third context is the struggle of women for their own voice and their own deserved place in both Western and non-Western settings.

At one level, the purpose of both essays is to make sense of the various encounters between "others," namely, two quite different encounters of the Jewish Jesus with two quite different non-Jewish women, and the violent encounters between nations and cultures at war as exemplified in the war between Croatians, Muslims, and Serbians in the Balkans. But our attempts to make sense of these encounters are guided also by the desire to *make a difference.* Theology serves mission. The encounters of Jesus with the Samaritan and Syrophoenician women are all about crossing boundaries and about mission across boundaries, and the purpose of the essay "Exclusion and Embrace" is to suggest new theological categories to help the church deal with conflicts between cultures.

Finally, in both essays theological and missional reflection is guided by the notion of "embrace." Embrace means more than giving "others" their due, even more than reconciliation. Embrace stands for reaching out to "others" and finding a place *within ourselves as individuals and cultures for "others" while still remaining ourselves.* More precisely, embrace stands for "a spacious heart." As the first essay's exegesis shows, Jesus' encounter with the Syrophoenician woman provides the most significant biblical example of such an enrichment by "others." This book is a call to open ourselves to the Spirit of God, the Spirit of mercy, justice, and truth; it is a call to help heal our world by embracing "others" as we remain true to ourselves.[1]

1

Spirit, Mercy, and the "Other"

Judith M. Gundry-Volf

The Gospel stories of Jesus' encounters with the Samaritan woman (John 4:1–42) and the Syrophoenician woman
(Mark 7:24–30; Matt. 15:21–28) can both be read as tales
about the inclusion of the "other" — about crossing the
boundaries caused by ethnic, religious, social, and gender
otherness and bringing about a new, inclusive community
of salvation. Exclusion is overcome in two radically different ways in these stories, so that they present us with
two different but complementary models for dealing with
a problem in our own world that is both urgent and complex. In John 4, the divine gift of the Spirit breaks down
barriers between people and leads to reconciliation and fellowship. In Mark 7 and Matthew 15, human insistence on
divine mercy, which is blind mercy, dramatically reverses a
pattern of exclusion.

Thanks go to Miroslav Volf and Young Lee Hertig for helpful interaction
on the multicultural dimensions of the biblical texts, and to Robert H.
Gundry for his comments on the earlier version of this essay.

Living Water

"How is it that you, a Jew, ask a drink of me, a woman of Samaria?" In this way the woman at the well answered Jesus when, wearied from a long journey, he bade her give him a drink of water. It was a simple request, yet at the same time an extremely problematic one. The evangelist explains why: "For Jews have no dealings with Samaritans" (John 4:9).[1] Either he had in mind the fact that Jews could contract ritual impurity by using a common vessel to draw water,[2] or that they avoided social contact in general with Samaritans, as also with Gentiles. Jews found plenty of religious reasons for such avoidance: the Samaritans, although they came to worship Yahweh, recognized only the Pentateuch as Scripture, and their holy mountain was Gerizim, not Zion (cf. Brown 1966:171–72).[3] The Jews regarded the Samaritans' Yahwism as a "thin veneer spread, for convenience, over an essential and deep-seated heathenism" (Gaster 1962:191). There was also a history of conflict between the two peoples. The Samaritans had impeded the Jews' restoration of Jerusalem after the Babylonian Exile and aided Syria in wars against the Jews. The Jews in turn had burned down the Samaritan temple on Gerizim in 128 B.C. Thus the hostility was mutual. All of this forms the background for the woman's question "How is it that you, a Jew, ask a drink of me, a woman of Samaria?" It was indeed an unlikely request — yet, for the reader of this story, one not unprepared for.

Already in the narrative Jesus has acted in disregard of expectations and taboos. He took the route from Judaea to Galilee less traveled by Jews, the one through Samaria (4:3–4).[4] Jews who wanted to avoid contact with Samaritans went the longer and more difficult way through Perea.

Jesus comes to the Samaritan city of Sychar (4:5). Not only does he not avoid Samaritan territory; he strikes up a conversation with one of the natives. Moreover, the native he engages in conversation is a woman. Jewish men were supposed to avoid contact with women, who were seen to pose a threat of seduction. Even conversation with one was dangerous: "Do not go to meet a loose woman, lest you fall into her snares.... [M]any have been misled by a woman's beauty" (Sir. 9:3–9).[5] This stereotypical view of women explains the disciples' shock when they return to the well: "They marveled that he was talking with a woman" (4:27). But, just as Jesus did not shun the Samaritans, so also he does not treat this woman as an obstacle in his path. For him she is not a sex object to be held at a distance. He is ready to join in conversation with her, as he does later, to enter a theological dialogue, as well as to share her water jar. Jesus' request for a drink of water, therefore, is deceptively simple. To make it he had to cross great gulfs — geographical, ethnic, religious, and gender.[6]

The Samaritan woman's question "How is it that *you* ask *me* for a drink?" shows that she recognized the barrier-breaking significance of Jesus' request. It struck her because it was so improbable. Furthermore, it must have struck her favorably. Here was a Jew who did not impose on her the Jewish stereotype of a Samaritan, someone with whom he wanted nothing to do. Here was a man who did not impose on her the stereotype of a woman. Her experience with men seems indeed to have been unfortunate: she had had five husbands, and the man she had now was not her husband (4:17–18).[7] She had doubtless experienced suffering in those relationships, possibly also unjust suffering. Her experience with Jesus was different. He pierced through the stereotypes and saw her as a woman who had come to draw water but was in need of much more than the water that Jacob's well could provide. Jesus addresses her need: "If you knew the gift of God, and who it is that is saying to you, 'Give me a drink,' you would have asked him, and he would have given you living water" (4:10).

What is the "living water"? The Samaritan woman takes it to be flowing water, or spring water (cf. 4:11), which was superior to water that collected through infiltration in a well. She understands that Jesus is claiming to give better water than the water of Jacob's well; therefore, he must know of a source of better, flowing water (4:11).[8] Most interpreters think that the woman is completely mistaken. The "living water" is not water that comes from a spring; rather, Jesus means the "water of life."[9] These are not really alternatives, however, for Jesus says that the living water that he gives "will become a spring of water welling up to eternal life" (4:14). Although the woman's understanding of living water is mistaken in a literal sense, it is true in a figurative sense: the living water has the superior qualities of spring water. As the story unfolds, those superior qualities become evident. Not only does the living water begin to well up in the Samaritan woman and her fellow Samaritans to eternal life as they believe in Jesus as the Savior of the world; the living water also overflows the boundaries dividing the figures in this story and envelops them in a new, inclusive fellowship. It is this reconciling power of the living water *between people* that deserves further attention.

The Samaritan woman needs this kind of living water. She had come to her people's well to draw water. But that water could not supply her deeper need. Indeed, Jacob's well itself symbolizes the need for reconciliation between people. It stands for the alienation between Samaritans and

Jews, for it is the well of the Samaritan patriarch that supplied him and the Samaritan community for generations (4:12), but whose water is inaccessible for a thirsty Jewish traveler with no vessel with which to draw (4:11). Jacob's well also symbolizes the Samaritan woman's alienation from her very own people. Note that she comes to draw water at the sixth hour, or in the middle of the day, counting from 6 A.M. She does not come in the morning or evening when others would be drawing water, but at the hottest time of the day.[10] She seems to be trying to avoid social contact. Jesus is alone at the well when she arrives. Perhaps she had been ostracized because of her irregular marital history, which included multiple remarriages and her current non-marital status.[11] Jacob's well thus stands for the bitter water of her marginalization.[12]

Jesus' spring, by contrast, is a symbol of the sweet water of inclusion. As the Samaritan woman experiences inclusion through Jesus' dismantling of ethnic, religious, and gender barriers, she begins to taste this water and then to thirst after it.[13] Her initial, reflex response to Jesus is filled with ethnic and religious pride. She is skeptical of his claim to have something better than the water from Jacob's well. "Sir, you have nothing to draw with, and the well is deep; where do you get that living water? Are you greater than our father Jacob, who gave us the well, and drank from it himself, and his sons, and his cattle?" (4:11–12). How is a weary and thirsty foreigner with no water jar going to provide something better than Jacob's well has done for generations?[14] Bultmann's (1971:132) explanation of the obstacle to the woman's believing in Jesus misses the dimension of presumed ethnic superiority. The obstacle is not simply that the Revealer is clothed in the form of a tired traveler, but that he is a Jew and that he challenges the Samaritan hero.[15]

At first the woman grasps onto traditional notions of ethnic and religious superiority.

Yet these are not finally satisfying. Jacob's well is reliable and familiar, but superior living water would relieve her of recurring thirst and the wearisome and lonely journey to the well. Further, Jesus' open and accepting manner has intrigued the woman. So she abandons her stance on Samaritan ethnic and religious superiority in favor of something that promises to be better: "Sir, give me this water, that I may not thirst, nor come here to draw" (4:15). Forget the paternal well! She will not be deprived of Jesus' spring.

Her hunch about Jesus and the living water receives further confirmation in the following dialogue. Jesus speaks with prophetic insight about the woman's life: "You have had five husbands; and he whom you now have is not your husband" (4:18). She concludes that Jesus is a prophet (4:19), for he told her all the things she had done (4:29, 39). Not only his insight, but also his compassion must have impressed her. Knowing all she had done, he did not reject her but reached out to her, a Samaritan, a woman, an outcast. Her estimation of Jesus grows. He is indeed greater than "our father Jacob," for he brings a new quality of life that alleviates her own physical and social suffering.

Indeed, it appears that he is the Coming One: he "told me all that I ever did. Can this be the Christ?" (4:29).[16] She shares the expectation that when the Messiah comes "he will show us all things" (4:25). She has seen Jesus demonstrate this ability. But it is surely not this ability in and of itself that suggests to the woman that Jesus is the Messiah. Rather, his declaration of all the things *she had done* is the critical indicator. He brings her deeds to the light, and she now stands completely exposed before the Revealer — yet she *stands!* And with outstretched arms he offers her the living water. Is not this the promised blessing, the messianic blessing of shalom?

The living water satisfies. The woman leaves her water jar at the well and goes back to the city (4:28). What need does she have for a water jar when she has drunk the living water that makes one never thirst again? She goes to her fellow Samaritans to tell them of this Jesus who offers something better than their patriarch Jacob. "Come, see the man...!" She brings this good news to the very people who had ostracized her. They too, like Jesus, know the things she had done, but unlike Jesus, they had rejected her. The ethnic bond was a thin veneer over a thick layer of alienation between her and her people. But when the living water flows, boundaries are traversed, social and gender boundaries as well as ethnic ones. The differences no longer separate. The woman regains a voice in her community, her witness is heard and believed, and her key role in the salvation of the Samaritans is recognized, as we find out in the climax to the story.

The Samaritans in the city listen to the woman's testimony, they heed her call to come and see, and they go out to Jesus to make the comparison themselves between the living water and the water of Jacob's well (4:28–30). And they too believe. They believe not just that Jesus is the Samaritan Messiah, the *Taheb*. They believe that he is the "Savior of the world" (4:39–42).[17] Ethnic and religious exclusivism is overcome once again. The reconciling power of the living water *between people* again comes to dramatic expression, for the city folk believe "because of the woman's testimony" (4:39).[18] The one whom they had marginalized has now become the one through whom they believe. Believing in Jesus is thus at the same time reconciliation between those who are estranged, and creation of inclusive fellowship.

In the climax to this story, where all boundaries are traversed through the inclusive power of the living water, the Samaritans press Jesus "to stay with them" (4:40). A Jewish traveler crossing through Samaria to Galilee ends up in the welcoming arms of his traditional antagonists. Samaritan skepticism — "How is it that you, a Jew, ask a drink of me, a woman of Samaria?" — has given way to "Christian" hospitality in the deepest sense. Jesus accepts their offer and stays two days with the Samaritans (4:40). "And many more believed because of his word" (4:41).[19] The entire story testifies that the gift of eternal life is experienced in the fellowship of those once estranged but now reconciled, and that that fellowship is an integral part of the gift itself.

New Worship of God

This new inclusive fellowship, which is possible through the new worship of God that Jesus brings, is the subject of the final part of his conversation with the Samaritan woman (4:19–24). She puts to him the question of the true worship of God: "Our fathers worshiped on this mountain; and you [Jews] say that in Jerusalem is the place where [one] ought to worship" (4:20). "This mountain" is Mount Gerizim, at the foot of which she and Jesus were standing; it is the traditional site of Jacob's well. The woman wants Jesus, who speaks with the authority of a prophet, to confirm that the Samaritans have the true worship of God, and the Jews do not. Gerizim and Jerusalem are mutually exclusive alternatives. Steeped in her own religious tradition, the woman can pose the question of true worship only in terms of "either/or."

The question of true worship and the way in which the

question is posed in terms of mutually exclusive alternatives is really a continuation of the discussion on water at the beginning of Jesus' conversation with the Samaritan woman. The water of Jacob's well represents Samaritan worship. Neyrey (1979:136) observes that in traditions concerning Jacob his well is portrayed as "itself the cipher for knowledge, cult and spirit." Here that well stands over against the living water that the Jewish Jesus has to offer, so that the woman sees herself forced to choose between Samaritan and Jewish cults. Thus "John's dialogue in chap. 4 intends the reader to link the well part of the discourse with the subsequent material on worship" (:136).

Jesus, however, "refuses to accept the alternative as such, but contrasts the present cultic division with the future" (Bultmann 1971:189). "The hour is coming when neither on this mountain nor in Jerusalem will you worship the Father" (4:21). The new, true worship of God will not be tied to any particular cult. "The hour is coming, and now is, when the true worshipers will worship the Father in spirit and truth. . . . God is spirit, and those who worship him must worship in spirit and truth" (4:23–24). The new worship of God is thus worship in the Spirit, who indwells both Samaritan and Jewish believers in Jesus. It is ethnically inclusive worship. For that matter, it is also gender inclusive and socially inclusive.

The hour of true worship has come with Jesus' gift of the living water, which is the Spirit (cf. 7:37–39).[20] Just as the water of Jacob's well is superseded by the living water that Jesus gives, so also the Samaritan cult and the Jewish cult are superseded by the new worship of God "in spirit and truth."[21] Jesus does not mean that true worship is essentially inward. Rather, it is the indwelling Spirit, not the external cult, that makes for true worship, so that both

Samaritans and Jews worship in truth not by virtue of the legitimacy of their cult but because they have been "born of the Spirit" (3:5). The answer to the woman's question, on which mountain ought one to worship God, is thus: on no mountain, but in spirit. Or: on any mountain — in spirit.

The Children's Bread

The story of Jesus and the Samaritan woman sits well with us. It portrays an admirable Jesus. He does not operate with stereotypes. He is open; he embraces people who are unlike him, even hostile to him. He does not try to squeeze them into a mold or demand their conformity to foreign ways for the enjoyment of salvation. He patiently draws them out to see and desire this marvelous gift. He breaks down the barriers that stand between people. He gives the living water, the Spirit, and the blessings of salvation roll down to all.

That is not, however, the same Jesus we encounter in Mark 7:24–30 and Matthew 15:21–28. These evangelists record an encounter of Jesus with another non-Jewish woman, the Syrophoenician, which is strikingly different from that with the Samaritan. In the story of the Syrophoenician woman, it seems that the barriers — ethnic, gender, socioeconomic, and political — between her and Jesus will in fact prevail, that no inclusion of the Gentiles is in sight. Only at the end, after Jesus himself and the disciples have reinforced these barriers, do they fall, through the Syrophoenician woman's own challenging of them.[22]

Jesus has withdrawn into the district of Tyre and Sidon. This was predominantly Gentile territory.[23] But he does not seek any mission activity among the Gentiles.[24] He wants

privacy. In Mark he retires to a house "and would not have
anyone know it" (7:24).[25]

Nevertheless, a woman hears about him and seeks him
out. She is "a Greek [Hellenist], a Syrophoenician by
birth" (Mark 7:26; cf. Matthew's "a Canaanite woman
from that region" 15:22). She is both Gentile by race and
Greek by culture. *Hellenis*, "hellenized person," refers to
someone who speaks Greek and is otherwise integrated
into Greek culture. The designation also suggests the
woman's socioeconomic rank, because Hellenization had
had the greatest impact among the upper class. When this
upper-class, Greek-speaking Gentile woman comes to a
Jewish Galilean wandering teacher and healer, as Theissen (1991:70) remarks, "Here two different 'social worlds'
meet."

From Jesus' standpoint as a Jewish carpenter by race and
by trade, the differences would have been sore points as
well. The inhabitants of Tyre are described by the Jewish
historian Josephus (*Ap* 1.13) as "notoriously our bitterest
enemies." There was a history of economic and political
oppression of Jews by the cities of Tyre and Sidon. The
Galilean backcountry and rural regions around Tyre, where
Jewish farmers could be found, produced most of the food
for the city dwellers. But the latter bought up and stored so
much of the harvest for themselves each season and during
times of crisis that the country folk did not have enough
(Galen 749f.). Tyre and Sidon also posed a political threat
to the Jews because the cities pursued a policy of territo-
rial expansion to the south and to the east, which at times
proved successful.[26] So when a Syrophoenician Hellenist
woman from this region seeks out help from Jesus, who
has deliberately withdrawn from the public eye, her mission
seems doomed from the start.

As the story unfolds, this impression is confirmed. Matthew's account brings this out most forcefully. The woman has to come out after Jesus and pursue him, shouting to get his attention.[27] She cries out, "Have mercy on me, O Lord, Son of David; my daughter is severely possessed by a demon" (Matt. 15:22). But her pathetic plea falls on deaf ears: "He did not answer her a word" (15:23). She, however, kept shouting out her request.[28]

First the disciples turn against her. They ask Jesus to "send her away, for she is crying after us" (15:23). She is a pest. Jesus responds, apparently to the disciples, with a justification for his ignoring her: "I was sent only to the lost sheep of the house of Israel" (15:24). Jesus senses a divinely given responsibility to Jews, but not to Gentiles such as the Syrophoenician woman. His mission, at least for now, is defined by ethnic boundaries.

The woman finally catches up to them. She "came and knelt before him" (15:25) in a position of worship. In this position she addresses him as "Lord" and pleads, "Help me!" (15:25). Still, her desperation does not affect Jesus. Surprisingly, even her worship of him as Lord[29] does not lead him to respond in a way befitting his role as divine helper. He is still operating with two mutually exclusive alternatives: If he is sent to the lost sheep of the house of Israel, then he is not sent to the Gentiles. Again, he formulates the possibility of a mission to the Jews and a mission to the Gentiles as alternatives: "It is not fair to take the children's bread and throw it to the dogs" (15:26). The "children" are the Jews, the children of Abraham. The "dogs" are the Gentiles. The term "dog" was used in a metaphorical sense for a Gentile.[30] If one throws the bread to the dogs, the children will be deprived. And, after all, it is the *children's* bread. In Mark the opposition is less stark.

The dogs will get the bread only *after* the children do: "Let the children first be fed, for it is not right to take the children's bread and throw it to the dogs" (Mark 7:27). Mark's version allows for a mission to the Gentiles following the mission to the Jews and thus presents the blessing of Jesus' itinerant ministry as not limited to one ethnic group.[31] But Matthew transforms "a reference to sequential priority into a flat refusal" (Gundry 1982:314). His Jesus does not even foresee the future inclusion of Gentiles.

By the figure of speech that Jesus uses he appears not just to refuse the Syrophoenician woman but to insult her. The epithet "dogs" for Gentiles had derogatory connotations; dogs roamed the streets scavenging for food, and the Jews considered them unclean animals (Michel 1964:1101–2). Further, if the economic oppression of Jews by Gentiles is conjured up by association through the term "bread," then Jesus' words could have a sarcastically insulting ring. Theissen suggests that Jesus may be using a familiar proverb that would have been understood to mean: "First let the poor people in the Jewish rural areas be satisfied. For it is not good to take poor people's food and throw it to the rich Gentiles in the cities" (1991:75). On the other hand, it is possible that Jesus' use of the stereotypical designation "dogs" for Gentiles is not pejorative. He could have in mind household pets rather than strays, because the dogs are explicitly pictured as eating by the table in the next verse and implicitly pictured in the context of the feeding of the children. The use of the diminutive *kynarion* may suggest the meaning "little dogs, puppies,"[32] which would also make the epithet nonpejorative. Yet the contrast between children and dogs remains. The woman is being told that she has no right to expect Jesus to help her.

In this story Jesus encounters the "other" but excludes

her. He does not see his mission as encompassing her. But the "other" will not let herself be excluded!

Resisting Exclusion

The Syrophoenician woman knocks down every obstacle in her path to making Jesus her Lord, the Helper of the Gentiles. She meets his stony silence with more pleading. With her own repeated requests for Jesus to have mercy, she drowns out the disciples' request for Jesus to send her away. She factually negates his exclusive mission to the Jews when she, a Gentile, calls him Lord and worships him. Finally, she cleverly turns his own maxim supporting exclusivism into an illustration of inclusivism in salvation.

Accepting the designation "dogs" for Gentiles, she turns it to the Gentiles' advantage in her illustration. The illustration is drawn from her domestic experience — mealtime around the table, at which even the lowliest members of her household receive nourishment. "Yes, Lord," she counters Jesus, "yet even the dogs under the table eat the children's crumbs" (Mark 7:28). In her maxim both the dogs and the children eat, and they eat simultaneously. She bests both the Matthean and the Markan Jesus: she denies both exclusivism and sequential priority based on ethnic identity. The Gentiles can have the bread of the messianic blessings, and they can have it now.

Jesus has the power to fulfill her request, she implies in Matthew's version of her illustration. The falling crumbs that the dogs eat come from "their masters' (*kyrion*) table" (Matt. 15:27). She has addressed Jesus as *Kyrie*, "Lord" (15:25). By implication, then, the falling crumbs from the lords' table must refer to the bread that Jesus, the Lord, gives. The "children's bread" is his to give. He must decide whether or not he will really withhold it from the Gentiles. She challenges him to rise up to a new, ethnically broadened sense of his mission and his Lordship. Although she does not point out the fact, how ironic it would be for Jesus to withhold the "children's bread" from a *child* for whom she is entreating Jesus' help, her own daughter, cruelly possessed by a demon. Jesus had shown appreciation for the need of the children in his maxim: the children ought to receive bread. She capitalizes on this appreciation by implicitly contrasting it with the "factual devaluation of the need of her own child" (Theissen 1991:80). Even a household pet fares better.

Blind Mercy

What was the source of the Syrophoenician woman's hope that Jesus would deliver her daughter, despite all the obstacles? What motivated her to persist in hope at every turn, to apply her ingenuity, her life experience, even her powerlessness as a woman by falling down at his feet and pleading for mercy, in pursuit of the miracle?

She does not appeal to any right. Jesus does not allow for any right of the Gentiles to the fruits of his mission, and she does not argue to the contrary. She accepts the position of "dogs" in contrast to "children." She cannot assume a position of strength over against Jesus. She is a woman, entreating for another woman, a double gender disadvantage in the context of male/female relations of the day. Even if she does come from a higher socioeconomic status than Jesus, this is more a disadvantage than an advantage for her, because Jesus would presumably identify her with the oppressors of her Jewish neighbors. Her ethnicity, her gender, her socioeconomic status — on none of these things can she build a case for Jesus' intervention.

Her appeal is rather to mercy. We see this in her body language: she came and fell at his feet, prostrated herself. We see it in her pleading: "Have mercy on me, O Lord, Son of David. . . . Lord, help me!" We see it also in her argumentation. She counters Jesus' assertion that the dogs ought not to get the children's bread with an assertion that nevertheless the dogs can expect mercy — the falling crumbs. Thus Gentiles can expect deliverance from the Son of David. How does she come to this conclusion? The woman does not meet in *Jesus* the grace that crosses ethnic boundaries. She concludes it from her domestic experience. The dogs around her own table certainly do not have the same status as her beloved daughter, and the food is not prepared for them. Yet they are fed just as her daughter is. Mercy is a principle by which a woman runs her household. If *she* operates this way every day, would not also the *Lord*, who is in a far better position to exercise his power mercifully? Viewing the situation from her own life context, the woman must have been stunned at Jesus' duty-bound reluctance to work a miracle for a Gentile.

But this does not become a "stone of stumbling" for her. She believed. She believes that divine mercy knows no bias. And she believes that Jesus will show this kind of mercy. As she expresses this faith in him, he also begins to believe. He, the one sent to the lost sheep of the house of Israel, can also do a miracle for a Gentile woman. He can extend help even to a Syrophoenician Hellenist, who belonged to his and his people's oppressors, for mercy is unbounded. Jesus rises up to her faith in him as Lord of Gentile as well as Jew, of oppressor as well as victim. When he marvels at her faith, exclaiming, "O woman, great is your faith!" (Matt. 15:28), he does so not as one who has simply tested her faith and approved it, but as one who is himself inspired by her faith.[33]

Jesus also performed a miracle for the Roman centurion, another Gentile, and marveled at his faith (Matt 8:5–13). Yet that incident does not force the issue of a Gentile mission, as does this one.[34] The Roman centurion too believed that Jesus could do a long-distance miracle: "Lord, my servant is lying paralyzed at home, in terrible distress. . . . I am not worthy to have you come under my roof; but only say the word, and my servant will be healed" (8:5–8). The centurion appeals to Jesus' unchallenged authority in hope of a miracle. He too finds an analogy in his own sphere of power: "For I am a man under authority, with soldiers under me; and I say to one, 'Go,' and he goes, and to another, 'Come,' and he comes, and to my slave, 'Do this,' and he does it" (8:9). Here Jesus sees no problem for his exclusive mission to the Jews in the fact that a Gentile is seeking help from him. Perhaps the reason is that the centurion has approached Jesus man to man, commander to commander. The commonality between them apparently bridges the ethnic gap. Jesus responds without hesitation to the centurion's faith (8:7, 13). But this ministry to a Gentile is not programmatic; a Gentile mission does not develop from it. The basis on which Jesus performs the miracle, namely, his unchallenged authority, does not imply the extension of his mission to Gentiles on a broad basis.

This was not so in the case of the Syrophoenician woman. Her kind of faith, faith in unbiased, undeserved mercy — the faith of the power*less*, not of the power*ful* — did not overshadow her ethnic and gender otherness but highlighted it. In the encounter with her, Jesus is faced squarely with the apparent contradiction between fulfilling this Gentile's request and his perceived mission to Israel alone. Yet when the powerless woman impresses on him the power of mercy that is not based on privilege through birth or deserts, Jesus' sense of his mission is expanded through this principle of mercy, the basis of her faith (cf. Wong 1992:91). In this light he senses how appropriate it is that Gentiles should experience the fruit of his work now. So finally Jesus says the word — "Be it done for you as you desire" — "and her daughter was healed instantly" (Matt. 15:28). Fittingly, her desire determined Jesus' action, for *she* rightly expected divine grace to be extended to the Gentiles.

The principle of blind mercy that intrudes into Jesus' understanding of his mission through the Syrophoenician woman does result, broadly speaking, in an extension of his mission to Gentiles. In Matthew, Jesus immediately goes to the Sea of Galilee, attracts great crowds, and heals many, so that the multitude "glorified the God of Israel" (15:29–31). This last statement identifies the crowds as Gentiles.[35] Jesus' aloofness and disinterest toward Gentiles that the Syrophoenician woman experienced have warmed to compassion and active concern, evident in his feeding of the four thousand (15:32–38). Surveying the throng, he says, "I have compassion on the crowd, because they have been with me now three days, and have nothing to eat, and I am unwilling to send them away hungry, lest they faint on the way" (15:32). Whereas "he did not answer her a word" (15:23), now he expresses words of compassion for the Gentiles. Whereas the disciples wanted Jesus to "send" the woman away, Jesus does not want to "send" the crowds away hungry.[36] Whereas he initially denied "bread" to the "dogs," here he feeds the four thousand Gentiles with "bread" and fish. Whereas Jesus intended that only the children "be satisfied," the multitude of Gentiles "are satisfied" at the miraculous feeding. Whereas there would not be bread for the children if it were thrown to the dogs, Jesus multiplies it, so there is now so much that seven baskets full of leftovers remain after the feeding.[37]

Jesus does not try to hide from the crowds in Gentile territory (as in Mark). He launches out to minister to them. Matthew's redaction of Mark emphasizes Jesus' intent to minister to Gentiles (Gundry 1982:310). Jesus embraces the Gentiles as part of his present mission field and thus shows the triumph of divine mercy over ethnically based exclusivism.

This triumph is portrayed as coming about through a Gentile woman's bold and persuasive insistence that God's mercy is not doled out along ethnic, gender, or sociocultural lines. The proof comes with Jesus' climactic exorcism of the demon from the Gentile girl. The woman's faith and Jesus' power provide models for overcoming the exclusion and rejection of the "other," for with the exorcism of the demon from the little girl's body, "the equally threatening demon of prejudice between the members of different nations and cultures was 'driven out.'" "The miracle would not consist [only] in healing someone far away, but in the overcoming of an equally divisive distance: the prejudice-based distance between nations and cultures, in which the divisive prejudices are not simply malicious gossip, but have a real basis in the social, economic, and political relationships between two neighboring peoples" (Theissen 1991:79–80). Finally, it should not go unmentioned that the Syrophoenician woman's challenging of exclusion through divine mercy and wrestling for the divine blessing was for the sake of a child, a powerless one, and for that child's liberation.

One day after having worked on this chapter, I left my office and was waiting outside for my husband to pick me up. I was standing on the curb at a place where there is a lot of foot traffic. It is a downtown neighborhood, not an upscale one, and people of all descriptions could be seen passing by. Some were well dressed; others had tattered clothes. There were people of all skin colors, students, business people, children, street people. I don't remember whether I was still thinking about Jesus and the Samaritan woman and the Syrophoenician woman when I saw a man approach me. He was black. He was very thin and his clothes were dirty. He looked me in the eye. His eyes were sad, but expectant. He asked me if I had a penny for him. "I'm a homeless person," he said. I was feeling nervous. The man had come close and was standing quite near, as near as a good acquaintance would. I had a good amount of cash in my wallet and was concerned about that. I wanted to give him some money, but didn't want to take my eyes off him while searching for it. I couldn't be sure he wouldn't pull out a weapon or grab my purse and run. When you live in greater Los Angeles such things enter your mind, especially if you are a woman. You know of stories, not just from the newspaper, but from your students, your friends. "I won't do you no harm," he assured me. I opened my purse and quickly pulled out some change. I put the coins in his open, thin, black hand. He lifted up his head and looked at me again, still standing close. "God bless you," he said. A gust of alcohol blew into my face as he spoke the words. Then he turned away, counting the money as he went. It was over. I was relieved. At that moment a car pulled up to the curb, my husband behind the wheel. I got in and was whisked away to my home on the edge of the city.

The next time that I thought about the Samaritan woman and the Syrophoenician woman, I saw the black man in my mind. He had come to me asking for just a

penny because he was thirsty, he needed a drink. The demon of his addiction possessed him and made him seek to
fulfill its desires. I gave him what he asked for, basically,
just a little bit more. That sent him away. I had felt the
barriers between us: he was a black man and I am a white
woman; he was a street person, I am an academician; he was
poor, I am rich by comparison. The stereotypes came without being invited. This man may be a threat to me; in any
case, he is not someone with whom I have anything to do.
No boundaries were crossed. No fellowship came about. No
living water was tasted. I just gave him some change, and
he went to buy his liquor. It was not the first bottle, and it
would not be the last. He would be thirsty again, until he
drinks the living water that wells up like a spring, the water of life that overflows the barriers. He went off without
any miracle of liberation. In fact, it was I who received the
blessing from him: "God bless you" were his parting words.

2

Exclusion and Embrace:
Theological Reflections in the Wake of
"Ethnic Cleansing"

Miroslav Volf

In the Gospels, Jesus tells a puzzling story about the unclean spirit who leaves a person, only to return with seven other spirits of an even more wicked character. The new state of the person is even worse than the old (see Matt. 12:45ff.). I am sometimes tempted to apply this story to the situation in Eastern Europe after the 1989 revolution. The demon of totalitarian communism has just been or is being exorcised, but worse demons seem to be rushing in to fill the empty house (Volf Spring 1991:78).

This is how I introduced a paper two years ago on the tasks of the churches in Central and Eastern Europe after the 1989 revolution. The paper was given at a conference of Third World theologians in Osijek, Croatia. Some six months later, the Evangelical Theological Faculty, which hosted the conference, had to flee to neighboring Slovenia; Osijek was being shelled day in and day out by Serbian forces. What during the conference had only seemed about to happen had in fact already taken place. New demons had possessed the Balkan house and were preparing their vandalistic and bloody feast, first in Croatia and then in Bosnia. Signs of their presence in other parts of Eastern Europe were less tangible but nonetheless real. As soon as the undivided "new Europe" appeared on the horizon, it seemingly vanished again into the thick smoke of the stubborn Balkan fire.

What are some of the key theological issues facing Christians in Central Eastern Europe, particularly in the Balkans? With the heat of the battle subsiding and attention no longer focused on killing or on surviving, two issues are at the forefront of people's minds. The first is *evil and sin:* how does one make sense of the vicious circle of hell — deep hatred and the baffling network of small and great evils that people inflict on each other? The second is *reconciliation:* how do we stop the killing and learn to live together after so much mutual hatred and bloodshed have shaped our common history? Both of these issues coalesce in the more abstract but fundamental question of *otherness* — of ethnic, religious, and cultural difference. In the Balkans this question is seldom posed in such abstract terms and is often not asked consciously at all, but it frames many other questions with which people are grappling daily.

Those whose theological palates long for some exotic fruit from foreign soil might be disappointed with my list. Are not these same issues surfacing everywhere in the world today? Am I not offering staple foods that can be found anywhere? My answer is yes, probably. But then as a theological chef I do not think this should bother me. My responsibility is not to tickle the palates of Western theological connoisseurs dulled by abundance and variety, but to fill the empty stomachs of people engaged in a bloody conflict. I have to prepare the food *they* need. Opinions of connoisseurs might be interesting and instructive, but nutritious value for the hungry is what matters. This is what it means to do contextualized theology. So my question will be, How do the issues of otherness, sin, and reconciliation look from the perspective of the social upheaval and ethnic conflict in the Balkans?

Much of my reflection on these issues took place as I was living and teaching in Osijek during the fall of 1992. By that time, the war in Croatia was over (or at least its first phase was[1]), but its traces were everywhere — broken windows, scarred facades, destroyed roofs, burned and desolated houses, a ruined economy, and, above all, many deep wounds in the hearts of the people. But the war was continuing with even greater brutality in the neighbors' courtyard.

As Croatians were watching the unabated Serbian aggression in Bosnia and trying to cope with the never-ending stream of refugees, they were reliving their own war inferno. There was much pride over their newly won statehood, even if it had had to be paid in blood. But there was even more trepidation about the future: When will the powerful aggressor be stopped and brought to justice? Would Croatians ever regain the lost territories and return to their villages and cities? If they did, how would they rebuild them? The feeling of helplessness and frustration, of anger and hatred, was ubiquitous.

From the beginning of the conflict I shared in the destiny of my people — first from afar, from Slovenia and from my home in California; then firsthand, when I arrived in Osijek for a prolonged stay. It was then that I was forced to start making sense of what I encountered. What I present here can best be described as a preliminary account of an exploration. This exploration would never have been undertaken and would have long since been given up had it not been for the powerful experience of the complex and conflicting social realities brought on by revolution and war. Experience goaded me on to explore, so I will not shy away from appealing to it here.

The Other

I was crossing the Croatian border for the first time since Croatia declared independence. State insignia and flags that were displayed prominently at the "gate to Croatia" were merely visible signs of what I sensed was an electrical charge in the air: I was leaving Hungary and entering Croatian space. I felt relief. In what used to be Yugoslavia, one was almost expected to apologize for being a Croat. Now I was free to be who I ethnically am.

Yet the longer I was in the country, the more hemmed in I felt. For instance, I sensed an unexpressed expectation to explain why as a Croat I still had friends in Serbia and did not talk with disgust about the backwardness of Byzantine-Orthodox culture. I am used to the colorful surrounding of multiethnicity. A child of a mixed marriage, I grew up in a city that the old Habsburg Empire had made into a meeting place of many ethnic groups, and I live in the tension-filled multicultural city of Los Angeles. But the new Croatia, like some jealous goddess, wanted all my love and loyalty; she wanted to possess every part of my being. "You must be Croat through and through, or you are not a good Croat," I could read between the lines of the large-lettered ethnic text that frequently met my eyes. "Croatia," I thought to myself, "will not be satisfied until it permeates everything in Croatia."

It is easy to explain this tendential *omnipresentia Croatiae in Croatia*. After forced assimilation under communist rule, it was predictable that the feeling of ethnic belonging would vigorously reassert itself. Moreover, the need to stand firm against a powerful and destructive enemy leaves little room for the luxury of divided loyalties. The explanations make sense, yet the unsettling question remains: does one not discover in Croatia's face at least some despised Serbian features? Has the enemy not captured Croatia's soul along with Croatia's soil? Serbian aggression has enriched the already oversized vocabulary of evil with the term "ethnic cleansing." Ethnic otherness is filth that needs to be washed away from the ethnic body, pollution that threatens the ecology of ethnic space. But, like many other countries, Croatia wants to be clean too — at least clean of its enemies, the Serbs! There is, of course, a world of difference in whether one suppresses otherness by social pressure to conform and emigrate, or even by discriminatory legislation, or whether one works to eliminate it with the destructive power of guns and fire. Is not the goal the same, however — a monochrome world, a world without the other?

During my stay in Croatia I read Jacques Derrida's reflections on contemporary Europe. He comments on his own European identity:

> I am European, I am no doubt a European intellectual, and I like to recall this, I like to recall this to myself, and why would I deny it? In the name of what? But I am not, nor do I feel, European in every part, that is, European through and through.... Being a part, belonging as "fully a part," should be incom-

patible with belonging "in every part." My cultural identity, that in the name of which I speak, is not only European, it is not identical to itself, and I am not "cultural" through and through, "cultural" in every part. (Derrida 1992:82f.).

The identity of Europe with itself, Derrida went on to say, is totalitarian. Indeed, Europe's past is full of the worst of violences committed in the name of European identity. Europe colonialized and oppressed, destroyed cultures and imposed its religion — all not only in the name of that glittering god named "gold," but also in the name of the exalted image of itself. It was not too long ago that Germany sought to conquer and exterminate in the name of its identity with itself (and Croatia participated in the project in its own way). Today, the Balkans are aflame in the name of Serbia's identity with itself. Identity without otherness — this is our curse!

The practice of ethnic and other kinds of "cleansing" in the Balkans forces us to place otherness at the center of theological reflection. The problem is, of course, not specific to the Balkans. The processes of integration in Europe place otherness high on the agenda. So do, for instance, the disintegration of the Soviet empire and the fragility of multiethnic and multireligious nations like India. The large framework for the problem is set by developments of planetary proportions. Modern means of communication and the emerging world economy have transformed our world from a set of self-contained tribes and nations into a global city. The unity of the human race is no longer an abstract notion. And the closer humanity's unity becomes, the more powerfully we experience its diversity. The "others" — persons of other culture, other religion, other economic status and so on — are not people we read about from distant lands. We see them daily on the screens in our living rooms; we pass by them on our streets. They are our colleagues and neighbors, some of them even our spouses. The others are among us; they are part of us. Yet they remain others, often pushed to the margins. How should we relate to them? Should we celebrate their difference and support it, or should we bemoan and suppress it? The issue is urgent. The ghettos and battlefields throughout the world testify indisputably to its importance.[2] It is not too much to claim that the future of not only the Balkans but of the whole world depends on how we deal with ethnic, religious, and gender otherness.

Liberation theologians taught us to place the themes of oppression and liberation at the center of theological reflection. They drew our attention to the God who is on the side of the poor and the oppressed, and the demands of God's people to be on the same side too (see Gutiérrez 1973). Nothing should make us forget these lessons, for the preferential option for the poor is rooted deeply in biblical traditions. Nevertheless, the categories of oppression and liberation are by themselves inadequate to address the Balkan conflict — or, indeed, the problems in the world at large today. The categories are, of course, almost tailor-made for both Croats and Serbs: each side perceives itself as oppressed by the other, and both are engaged in what they believe to be the struggle for liberation. Unless one is prepared to say that one side is completely right and the other wrong, however, this is precisely where the problem lies.

Categories of oppression and liberation provide combat gear, not a pin-striped suit or a dinner dress; they are good for fighting, but not for negotiating or celebrating. Even assuming that the one side is right and the other wrong, what happens when the fight is over and (we hope) the right side wins? One still faces the question of how the liberated oppressed can live together with their conquered oppressors. "Liberation of the oppressors" is the answer that the "oppression-liberation" schema suggests. But is it persuasive? The categories of oppression and liberation seem ill-suited to bring about the resolution of conflicts between people and people groups. I suggest that the categories of "exclusion and embrace" as two paradigm responses to otherness can do a better job. They need to be placed at the center of a theological reflection on otherness, an endeavor I would like to term a "theology of embrace."

A theology of embrace would, however, amount to a betrayal both of God and oppressed people if it were pursued in such a way as to marginalize the problems of oppression and liberation. Rather, we need to see oppression and liberation as essential dimensions of exclusion and embrace, respectively. Those who are oppressed and in the need of liberation are often "the others." Almost invariably the oppressed do not belong to the dominant culture of the oppressors, but are persons or people groups of other race, gender, or religion. To embrace others in their otherness must mean freeing them from oppression and giving them space to be themselves. Anything else is either a hypocritical tap on the shoulders or a deadly "bear hug." Thus the question must never be whether one should struggle against oppression, but rather what theological categories are most adequate to accomplish the task.

I will address the issue of otherness first by looking at the nature of Christian identity. This will provide a platform from which to talk about sin as exclusion and about salvation as embrace. At the outset I have to beg for indulgence.

Within the confines of a single essay I am able neither to
ground the theology of embrace sufficiently in trinitarian
theology and Christology nor to develop it in any detail. In
particular, I am unable to address the important questions
of how embrace is related to justice and truth or how exclusion and embrace might differ when applied to individuals
and groups.

Aliens

In his reminiscences entitled *From the Kingdom of Memory*,
Elie Wiesel (1990:59–60) defines the stranger as "someone who suggests the unknown, the prohibited, the beyond;
he seduces, he attracts, he wounds — and he leaves. . . . The
stranger represents what you are not, what you cannot be,
simply because you are not *he*. . . . The stranger is *the other.*
He is not bound by your laws, by your memories; his
language is not yours, nor his silence."

How should we respond to the strange world of the
other? In answering this question, Christians will have to
reflect on their own identity as strangers.

From the inception of the Christian church, otherness
was integral to Christian ethnic and cultural identity (see
Feldmeier 1992). Toward the end of the New Testament
period, Christians came to designate themselves explicitly
as "aliens and exiles" (1 Pet. 2:11) (Stählin 1967:30). By
the second century these metaphors became central to their
self-understanding. They saw themselves as heirs to the
people of God: Abraham was called to go from his country, his kindred, and his father's house (Gen. 12:1); his
grandchildren and the children of his grandchildren became
"strangers in the land of Egypt" (Lev. 19:34); the nation
of which he and Sarah were foreparents lived as exiles in

the Babylonian captivity. And even when they lived securely in their own land, Jahweh their God expected them to be different from nations that surrounded them.

However, at the root of Christian self-understanding as aliens and exiles lies not so much the story of Abraham and his posterity as the destiny of Jesus Christ, his mission and his rejection, which brought him to the cross. "He came to his own home, and his own people received him not" (John 1:11). He was a stranger to the world because the world into which he came was estranged from God. And so it is with his followers. "When a person becomes a believer, then he moves from the far country to the vicinity of God.... There now arises a relation of reciprocal foreignness and estrangement between Christians and the world" (Stählin 1967:29). Christians are born of the Spirit (John 3:8) and are therefore not "from the world" but, like Jesus Christ, "from God" (John 15:19). It is not at the disposal of Christians whether to be alien in their own culture. The "difference" from one's own culture — from the concrete "world" one inhabits — is essential to the Christian's cultural identity.

But why be different? Simply for the sake of difference? Even that is progress in a world without the other. Belonging without distance destroys: I affirm my identity as Croatian and want either to shape everyone in my own image or eliminate them from my world. So why not dirty the walls of a monochrome culture with some spiteful, colorful graffiti? There is a value in difference even simply as difference. Yet the difference will remain sterile if it is nothing but a protest gesture. It might also turn into its very opposite. If belonging without distance destroys, distance without belonging isolates: I deny my cultural identity as Croatian and draw back from my own culture. But more often than not, I become trapped in the snares of counter-dependence. I deny my Croatian identity only to affirm even more forcefully my identity as a member of this or that anti-Croatian sect. And so, as the "positive fusion" is substituted by "negative fusion," an isolationist "distance without belonging" slips into a destructive "belonging without distance." Difference from a culture must never degenerate into a simple flight from that culture. Rather, to be alien and exile must be a way of living *in* a culture and *for* a culture. In biblical terminology, the kingdom of God is not *of* this world, but it is *in* this world and *for* this world. Distance must involve belonging as belonging must involve distance.

Given, then, the need for interpenetration of distance and belonging, what is the positive purpose of the distance? The category of "new creation" sets us on the trail leading to an answer. In a key passage about the nature of Christian existence, Paul writes: "So if anyone is in Christ, there is a new creation" (2 Cor. 5:17 NRSV). The rebirth of a person by the Spirit is nothing less than an anticipation of the eschatological new creation of God, a gathering of the whole people of God and of all the cultural treasures that have been dispersed among the nations. By the Spirit, that future universal event becomes a concrete reality in each believer.

One consequence of the re-creation of a person by the Spirit is that the person can no longer be thought of apart from the rich and complex reality of the new creation. The Spirit sets a person on the road toward becoming what one might call a "catholic personality," a personal microcosm of the eschatological new creation. Catholic personality is a personality enriched by otherness, a personality that is what it is only because all differentiated otherness of the new creation has been reflected in it in a particular way. The distance from my own culture that results from being born by the Spirit does not isolate me, but *creates space in me for the other*. Only in distance can I be enriched, so that I, in turn, can enrich the culture to which I belong.

Because everything belongs partly to a catholic personality, a person with catholic personality cannot belong to any one thing totally. The only way to belong is with distance. This distance from any particular reality — from any particular person and culture — that exists for the sake of transcending the exclusion of all other reality from that person's identity might be called "catholic foreignness." Christians are not simply aliens to their own culture; they are aliens that are at home in every culture because they are open to every culture. Something of this catholic foreignness might have been in the mind of the anonymous author of the Epistle to Diognetus when he wrote, "every foreign land is their fatherland and every fatherland is a foreign land" (Meecham 1949:81).

The notion of the catholic personality avoids exclusivism because each person has become a particular reflection of the totality of others. At the same time, it transcends indifferent relativism. Each does not simply affirm the otherness as otherness, but seeks to be enriched by it. But should a catholic personality integrate all otherness? Can one feel at home with everything in every culture? With murder, rape, and destruction? With nationalistic idolatry and ethnic cleansing? Any notion of catholic personality that was capable of only integrating but not of discriminating would be grotesque. For there are incommensurable perspectives that stubbornly refuse to be dissolved in a peaceful synthesis, and there are evil things that we should stubbornly resist to integrate into our personalities (see Mouw 1987:114ff.).

The practice of exclusion cannot be given up. The biblical category for it is "judgment." This brings us to the second positive purpose of the distance.

Distance that results from being born by the Spirit — catholic foreignness — entails *a judgment not only against a monochrome character of one's own culture but also against evil in every culture.* The new creation that an authentic catholic personality should anticipate is not an indiscriminate affirmation of the present world. Such an affirmation would be the cheapest of all graces, and hence no grace at all — not toward the perpetrators of evil, nor, of course, toward their many victims. There can be no new creation without judgment, without the expulsion of the devil and the beast and the false prophet (Rev. 20:10), without the swallowing up of the night by the light and of death by life (Rev. 21:4; 22:5). (See Volf 1991:120f.) The notion of catholic foreignness therefore necessarily involves a conflict with the world: the struggle between truth and falsehood, between justice and arbitrariness, between life and death (see Moltmann 1989:226; cf. idem December 1989:528–36). Distance from a culture that rebirth by the Spirit creates is a judgment against the evils of a culture. It creates space for the struggle against the various demons that assault it. A truly catholic personality must be an *evangelical* personality — a personality transformed by the Spirit of the new creation and engaged in the transformation of the world.

Does not talk about demons and darkness return us to the exclusion that the notion of the catholic personality should have overcome? Indeed, does not the notion of catholic personality presuppose exclusion because it rests not only on belonging but also on distance? The best way to tackle these questions is to look at the significance of "centrality." It seems rather obvious that when talking about identity one cannot do without a center; otherwise, the talk of difference and its being internal to oneself makes no sense. The difference is internal to what? Jacques Derrida, who is not known to be graceful toward what he calls "hegemonic centrality," recognizes as much when he insists that self-difference "would gather this center [the human center of an individual], relating it to itself, only to the extent that it would open it up to" the divergence from itself.[3] Derrida cannot give up the center, for then the difference would remain everywhere and nowhere. The center seems to function, however, only as a precondition for openness for the other, as a contentless container of difference.

But if the self is not a center organizing the difference, but merely a container of the difference, does one not end up — exactly contrary to Derrida's intention — with a "melting pot" (or some chaotic "salad bowl")? The lesser trouble with the melting pot is that it never existed. The greater trouble is that it dissolves the difference. The identity with oneself — a personal centeredness — must be preserved for the sake of difference.[4] My being centered in distance from the other is not a negative act of exclusion, but a creative act of separation. The Book of Genesis rightly describes creation as successive divine acts of separation (see 1:3ff.). Because I and the other can be constituted in our mutual otherness only by separation, no genuine openness to the other is possible without it. This is why the encounter with a stranger is creative only if, as Elie Wiesel (1990:73) puts it, you "know when to step back."[5]

In the case of Christians, superimposed on the center that creates their human identity is another center that creates their *Christian* identity. Emergence of this new center is also an act of creation — the new creation — and it takes place through separation. But why this new center? Why the additional separation? Because a human center is not an impersonal axis, but a personal self — a heart — that cannot exist without a "god," without a framework of meaning and value. The god of the self is the doorkeeper who decides about the fate of the otherness at the doorsteps of the heart. To embrace a Christian God does not mean to place a doorkeeper at the entrance of one's heart that was without one before, but to *re*place the one doorkeeper with another. One cannot get rid of one's gods; one can only change them. And when one thinks one has gotten rid of them, a restless demon who wanders through waterless regions looking for a resting place, but finds none, has already taken their place (see Matt. 12:43). So the question is not whether one has a doorkeeper, but who the doorkeeper is and how the doorkeeper relates to otherness. Does the Christian doorkeeper prohibit anything non-Christian from entering in?

There are two injunctions that persistently surface in the Bible. One is to have no strange gods; the other is to love strangers. The two injunctions are interrelated: one should love strangers in the name of the one triune God, who loves strangers. This triune God is the center that regulates a Christian's relationship to otherness, a doorkeeper who opens and closes the door of the self.[6] To be a Christian does not mean to close oneself off in one's own identity and advance oneself in an exemplary way toward what one is not. It means rather to be centered on this God — the God of the other — and participate in *God's* advance toward where God and God's reign is not yet. Without such centeredness, it would be impossible either to denounce the practice of exclusion or demand the practice of embrace.

Exclusion

What strikes one immediately in the Balkan war is the naked hate, a hate without enough decency — or shall we say hypocrisy? — to cover itself up. Not that hate is unique to this conflict. Most wars feed on hate, and the masters of war know how to manufacture it well. It is the proportions of the Balkan hate and its rawness right there on the fringes of what some thought to be civilized Europe that cause us to stagger. Think of the stories of soldiers making necklaces out of the fingers of little children! Never mind whether they are true or not; that they are being told and believed suffices. The hate that gives rise to such stories and wants to believe them is the driving force behind the ruthless and relentless pursuit of exclusion known as ethnic cleansing. This is precisely what hate is — an unflinching will to exclude, a revulsion for the other.

It might be that the most basic sin is pride, though this way of defining sin does not seem to capture with precision the experiences of most women (see Plaskow 1980; Hampson 1986:46–60). But I doubt that it is helpful to go about reducing all sins to their common root (see Moltmann 1992:127); the Bible at any rate does not seem to be interested in such a business. I will not pursue here the search for the one basic sin, but will indicate a fundamental way of conceiving sin: *sin as exclusion.*[7] For those who are interested in exploring the connection between exclusion and pride, one could point out that exclusion, which is a form of the contempt toward the other, might be considered "the reverse side of pride and its necessary concomitant in a world in which self-esteem is constantly challenged by the achievements of others" (Niebuhr 1961:211).

One of the advantages of conceiving sin as exclusion

is that it names as sin what often passes as virtue, especially in religious circles. In the Palestine of Jesus' day, "sinners" were primarily social outcasts, people who practiced despised trades, those who failed to keep the Law as interpreted by the religious establishment, and Gentiles and Samaritans. A pious person had to be separate from them; their presence defiled because they were defiled. Jesus' table fellowship with social outcasts, a fellowship that belonged to the central features of his ministry, turned this conception of sin on its head: *the real sinner is not the outcast but the one who casts the other out.* As Walter Wink writes, "Jesus distinguishes between those falsely called sinners — who are in fact victims of an oppressive system of exclusion — and true sinners, whose evil is not ascribed to them by others, but who have sinned from the heart (Mark 7:21)" (Wink 1992:115–16). Sin is not so much a defilement but a certain form of *purity* — the exclusion of the other from one's heart and one's world. In the story of the prodigal son, the sinner was the elder brother — the one who withheld an embrace and expected exclusion. Sin is a refusal to embrace the others in their otherness and a desire to purge them from one's world, by ostracism or oppression, deportation or liquidation.

The exclusion of the other is an exclusion of *God.* This is what one can read between the lines of the story of the prodigal son. The departure of the younger brother from the father's home was an act of exclusion. He wanted his father — and maybe his brother too — out of his world. Yet in his life of exclusion, in the far country, he was closer to the father than was his older brother who remained at home. For like the father, he longed for an embrace. His older brother kept the father in his world, but excluded him from his heart. For the older brother, an act of exclusion demanded retaliatory exclusion. But for the father, an act of exclusion called for an embrace. By excluding his younger brother, the older brother excluded the father who longs for an embrace.

But did not *both* brothers exclude the father? Are they not *both* sinners? Are they not both *equally* sinners? This brings us to the problem of the universality of sin.

From a distance things look fairly simple in the Balkan war: Croatians (and Muslims) are the victims, and Serbians are the aggressors. Has any city in Serbia been destroyed, any of its territories occupied? The macro-picture of the conflict is clear, and it does not seem likely that anything will ever change it. I approached the clear contours of this picture with a pre-reflective expectation that the victim is innocent and the oppressor guilty. This natural presumption was aided by my belonging to the victimized group. I had, of course, never doubted that Croatians share some blame for the outbreak of the war (just as I never doubted that only Croatia's renunciation of sovereignty would have prevented the conflict from breaking out in the first place). But I expected Croatians to be more humane victims. At night in Osijek, I would hear explosions go off and know that another house or a shop of a Serb who did not emigrate had been destroyed, and rarely was anyone brought to justice. Refugees, those who were victimized the most, looted trucks that brought them help; they were at war with *each other*. Are these simply necessary accompaniments of a war? If so, they prove my point: the more closely one looks at the picture, the more the line between the guilty and the innocent blurs and all that one sees is an intractable maze of small and large brutalities. I was tempted to exclaim: "All are evil, equally evil!" But then I heard those same words broadcast by the Serbian propaganda machine.

The logic was simple: If evildoers are everywhere, then the violence of the aggressor is no worse than the violence of the victim. All are aggressors and all are victims. Placing the micro-picture of the maze of evil so close to our eyes was calculated to remove the macro-picture of aggression and suffering from our field of vision.

Christian theology has traditionally underlined the universality of sin. "All have sinned and fall short of the glory of God," writes the apostle Paul, echoing some central Old Testament passages (Rom. 3:9ff.). In the bright light of the divine glory, stains of injustice appear on all human righteousness, and blemishes of narcissism, indifference, and sometimes hate appear on all human love. In addition to freeing us "from delusions about the perfectibility of ourselves and our institutions" (Wink 1992:71), the doctrine of the universality of sin pricks the thin balloons of self-righteousness of aggressor and victim alike and binds them in the solidarity of sin, thus preparing the way for reconciliation. This is why the doctrine of the universality of sin should not be given up.

However, if all are sinners, are all sins equal? Reinhold Niebuhr, who in our century most powerfully restated the doctrine of the universality of sin, thought so. But he sought to balance the equality of sin with the inequality of guilt (Niebuhr 1961:222ff.). If one affirms the equality of sin, then such a balancing act becomes unavoidable. But why assert the equality of sin in the first place? From "all are sinners" *does not* follow "all sins are equal" (Wolf 1956:240). Aggressors' destruction of a village and refugees' looting of a truck are equally sin, but they are not equal sins. The equality of sins dissolves all concrete sins in an ocean of undifferentiated sinfulness. This is precisely what the prophets and Jesus did not do. Their judgments are not general but specific; they do not condemn everyone and anyone, but the rich and mighty who oppress the poor and crush the needy The sin of driving out "the other" from their possessions, from their work, from their means of livelihood, the sin of pushing them to the margins of society and beyond weighs high on the scales of the rich and mighty. How could there be universal solidarity in *this* sin? The mighty are the sinners, and the weak are the sinned against. Even if all people sin, not all sin equally. To deny this would be to insult all those nameless heroes who refused to participate in power acts of exclusion and had the courage to embrace the other, even at the risk of being ostracized or imprisoned. The uprightness of these people demands that we talk about sin concretely (see Moltmann 1992:126).

But if we always speak of sin concretely — if we speak of it only in the plural — do we not reduce sin to sinful acts and intentions? Is this not too shallow a view of sin? And does it not lead to unhealthy and oppressive moralizing? The answer would be yes, if it were not for the *transpersonal dimension of sin and evil.*

"Eruption" might be a good word to describe the conflict in the Balkans. I am thinking here less of the suddenness by which it broke out than of its insuppressible power. It does not seem that anybody is in control. Of course, the big and strategic moves that started the conflict and that keep it going are made in the centers of intellectual, political, and military power. But there is way too much will for brutality among the common people. Once the conflict started, it seemed to trigger an uncontrollable chain reaction.[8] These were decent people, helpful neighbors. They did not, strictly speaking, *choose* to plunder and burn, rape and torture — or secretly enjoy these. A dormant beast in them was awakened from its uneasy slumber. And not only in them: the motives of those who set out to fight against the brutal aggressors were self-defense and justice, but the beast in others enraged the beast in them. And so the moral barriers holding the beast in check were broken, and it went after revenge. In resisting evil, people were trapped by it. After World War II, Carl Gustav Jung (1964:198) wrote, "It is a fact that cannot be denied: the wickedness of others becomes our own wickedness because it kindles something evil in our own hearts." Evil engenders evil, and like pyroclastic debris from the mouth of a volcano, it erupts out of aggressor and the victim alike.

In a fascinating book, *Engaging the Powers*, Walter Wink (1992:33–104) accesses the problem of the power of evil by looking at what he calls the "Powers" and their perversion into the "Domination System." The Powers, he claims, are neither simply human institutions and structures nor an order of angelic (or demonic) beings. They are both institutional and spiritual; they "possess an outer, physical manifestation . . . and an inner spirituality or corporate culture" (Wink Nov./Dec. 1992:17). The Powers are essentially good, but when they became "hell-bent on control," Wink claims, they degenerate into the Domination System. This System itself is neither only institutional nor only spiritual; rather, the "forces of this present darkness" (see Eph. 6:2) are the interiority of warped institutions, structures, and systems that oppress people. I will modify Wink's terminology and substitute the "Exclusion System" for his "Domination System," for as a rule the purpose of domination is to exclude others from scarce goods, whether they are economic, social, or psychological. But Wink is right that it is through the operation of the *System* that the power of evil imposes itself so irresistibly on people. Caught in the System of exclusion, as if in some invisible snare, people begin to behave according to its perverted logic. Should we call this anything else but "possession"?

Yet persons cannot be reduced to the System. The System needs persons to make it "breathe" with the spirit of evil, and persons can escape the logic of the System, as the noble history of resistance demonstrates. So if people do acquiesce, it is not because the System forces them to acquiesce, but because there is something in their souls that resonates with the logic of exclusion. Could the culprit be the desire for identity — the instinctive will to be oneself — that is written into the very structure of our selves, as Wolfhart Pannenberg has recently suggested (1991:298f.)? The will to be oneself is essentially healthy, of course. Yet it always carries within it the germs of its own illness. To remain healthy, the will to be oneself needs to make the will to be the other part of itself. And so, because the other must become part of who we are as we will to be ourselves, a tension is built into the desire for identity. It is the antipodal nature of the will to be oneself that makes the slippage into exclusion so easy. The power of sin from without — the Exclusion System — thrives on both the power and the powerlessness from within, the irresistible power of the will to be oneself and the powerlessness to resist the slippage into exclusion of the other.

The desire for identity could also explain why so many people let themselves be sinned against so passively — why they let themselves be excluded. It is not because they do not have the will to be themselves, but because one can satisfy that will *by surrendering to the other*. Their problem is not so much exclusion of the other from their will to be oneself, but a paradoxical exclusion of their *own* self from the will to be oneself (what in feminist theology is called "diffusion of the self"). I call this exclusion a "problem," not a "sin," for it often comes about as a result of introjected acts of exclusion that we suffer.[9] Sin "is lurking at the door" when the introjected exclusion of ourselves by others results in our exclusion of the others — when we start looking for everything dark, inferior, and culpable in them. Like Cain, we then become ready to kill the otherness of the other.

Embrace

What do we do against the terrible sin of exclusion that lurks at our door or has already entered our soul? How do we master it? Is there a way out of the circle of exclusion to an embrace? The tragedy of the Balkan situation is that very few people seem to be asking these questions. Vengeance is on everybody's mind. Serbs want to avenge the slaughter of their compatriots in World War II and to repay others for their injured sense of national pride during the postwar years. Croatians and Muslims want revenge for Serbian atrocities, some from the present war and some from the previous one, and for their economic exploitation. And the greater their success at revenging themselves, the more Serbs feel justified in their aggression. An evil deed will not be owed for long; it demands an instant repayment in kind. Vengeance, as Hannah Arendt (1958:240f.) wrote in *The Human Condition,* "acts in the form of reacting against an original trespassing, whereby far from putting an end to the consequences of the first misdeed, everybody remains bound to the process, permitting the chain reaction contained in every action to take its unhindered course; ... [vengeance] encloses both doer and sufferer in the relentless automatism of the action process, which by itself need never come to an end." The endless spinning of the spiral of vengeance has its own good reasons that are built into the very structure of our world. If our deeds and their consequences could be undone, revenge would not be necessary. The undoing, if there were will for it, would suffice. But our actions are irreversible. Even God cannot change them. And so the urge for vengeance or for punishment seems irrepressible. Arendt called this "the predicament of irreversibility" (:237). The only way out of it, she insisted, was through an act of *forgiveness.*

Yet forgiveness is precisely what seems impossible. Deep within the heart of every victim, hate swells up against the perpetrator. The Imprecatory Psalms seem to come upon their lips much more easily than the prayer of Jesus on the cross. If anything, they would rather pray, "Forgive them not, Father, for they knew what they did" (Abe Rosenthal). If the perpetrators were repentant, forgiveness would come more easily. But repentance seems as difficult as forgiveness. It is not just that we do not like being wrong, but that almost invariably the other side has not been completely right either. Most confessions, then, come as a mixture of repentance and aggressive defense or even lust for revenge (Jung 1964:240). Both the victim and the perpetrator are imprisoned in the automatism of exclusion, unable to forgive or repent and united in a perverse communion of mutual hate.

In the Imprecatory Psalms, the torrents of rage have been allowed to flow freely, channeled only by the robust structure of a ritual prayer (see Barth 1966:43ff.: Gerstenberger 1983:61–77). Strangely enough, it is they that point to a way out of the slavery of hate to the freedom of forgiveness. For the followers of the crucified Messiah, their main message is: hate belongs before God, not in a reflectively managed and manicured form of a confession, but as a pre-reflective outburst from the depths of our being. Hidden in the dark chambers of our hearts and nourished by the system of darkness, hate grows and seeks to infect everything with its hellish will to exclusion. In the light of the justice and love of God, however, hate recedes, and the seed is planted for the miracle of forgiveness. Forgiveness flounders because I exclude the enemy from the community of humans and exclude myself from the community of sinners. But no one can be in the presence of God for long without overcoming this double exclusion, without transposing the enemy from a sphere of monstrous inhumanity into the sphere of common humanity and oneself from the sphere of proud innocence into the sphere of common sinfulness. When one knows that the torturer will not eternally triumph over the victim, one is freed to rediscover the torturer's humanity and imitate God's love for that person. And when one knows that the love of God is greater than all sin, one is free to see oneself in the light of the justice of God and so rediscover one's own sinfulness.

Yet even when the obstacles are removed, forgiveness cannot simply be presumed (see McClendon 1986:224). It always comes as a surprise, at least to those who are not ignorant of the ways of men and women. Forgiveness *is* an outrage, not only against the logic of the Exclusion System but also "against straight-line dues-paying morality," as Lewis Smedes (1984:124) puts it. The perpetrator *deserves* unforgiveness. When forgiveness happens, there is always a strange, almost irrational, otherness at its very heart, even when we are aware that, given the nature of our world, it is wiser to forgive than to withhold forgiveness. Could it be that the word of forgiveness that must be uttered in the depths of our being, if it is uttered at all, is an echo of Another's voice?

Forgiveness is the boundary between exclusion and embrace. It heals the wounds that the power-acts of exclusion

have inflicted and breaks down the dividing wall of hostility. But it leaves a distance, an empty space between people
that allows them either to go their separate ways in what is
called "peace" or fall into each other's arms.

"Going one's own way" — a civilized form of exclusion — is what the majority of the people in the Balkans
contemplate in their most benevolent and optimistic mo-
ments. "Too much blood was shed for us to live together,"
I heard almost every time I participated in conversations
about what might happen after the clamor of battles dies
down. Never mind geographic proximity, never mind the
communication lines that connect us, our similar languages,
our common history, our interdependent economies, the
complex network of friendships and relations created by the
years of living with each other and making love to each
other! A clear line will separate "them" from "us." They will
remain "they," and we will remain "we," and we will never
include "them" when we speak of "us." We will be clean of
the others and identical with ourselves. And so there will be
peace among us. What muddies this clean calculation is the
fact that the war broke out in the name of Serbian identity with itself. By what magic does one hope to transform
exclusion from a cause of war into an instrument of peace?

The only way to peace is through embrace — that is,
after the parties have forgiven and repented, for without
forgiveness and repentance, embrace is a masquerade. An
embrace involves always a double movement of *aperture* and
closure. I open my arms to create space in myself for the
other. The open arms are a sign of discontent at being myself only and of desire to include the other. They are an
invitation to the others to come in and feel at home with
me, to belong to me. In an embrace I also close my arms
around the others — not tightly, so as to crush and assim-

ilate them forcefully into myself, for that would not be an embrace but a concealed power-act of exclusion; but gently, so as to tell them that I do not want to be without them in their otherness. I want them to remain independent and true to their genuine selves, to maintain their identity and as such become part of me so that they can enrich me with what they have and I do not (Wiesel 1990:61). An embrace is a "sacrament" of a catholic personality. It mediates and affirms the interiority of the other in me, my complex identity that includes the other, a unity with the other that is both maternal (substantial) and paternal (symbolic)[10] — and still something other than either.[11]

Why should I embrace the other? The answer is simple: because the others *are* part of my own true identity. I cannot live authentically without welcoming the others — the other gender, other persons, or other cultures — into the very structure of my being. For I am created to reflect the personality of the triune God. The Johannine Jesus says: "The Father is in me and I am in the Father" (John 10:38). The one divine person is not that person only, but includes the other divine persons in itself; it is what it is only through the indwelling of the other. The Son is the Son because the Father and the Spirit indwell him; without this interiority of the Father and the Spirit, there would be no Son. Every divine person *is* the other persons, but is the other persons in his or her own particular way. Analogously, the same is true of human persons created in the image of God. Their identity as persons is conditioned by the characteristics of other persons in their social relations. The others — other persons or cultures — are not filth that we collect as we travel these earthly roads. Filth is rather our own monochrome identity, which is nothing else but the sin of exclusion at cognitive and voluntative levels —

a refusal to recognize that the others have *already* broken in through the enclosure of our selves and unwillingness to make a "movement of effacement by which the self makes itself available to others" (Ricoeur 1992;168). In the presence of the divine Trinity, we need to strip down the drab gray of our own self-enclosed selves and cultures and embrace others so that their bright colors, painted on our very selves, will begin to shine.

But how do the bright colors shine when the Exclusion System is dirtying us incessantly with its drab gray paint? How do we overcome our powerlessness to resist the slippage into exclusion? We need the energies of the *Spirit of embrace* — the Spirit who "issues from the essential inward community of the triune God, in all the richness of its relationships," who lures people into fellowship with the triune God and opens them up for one another and for the whole creation of God (Moltmann 1992: 219). The Spirit of embrace creates communities of embrace — places where the power of the Exclusion System has been broken and from where the divine energies of embrace can flow, forging rich identities that include the other.

Notes

Introduction

1. For a more comprehensive theological reflection on identity and otherness, see Miroslav Volf, *Exclusion and Embrace: A Theological Exploration in Identity, Otherness, and Reconciliation* (Nashville: Abingdon Press, 1996).

1. Spirit, Mercy, and the "Other"

1. A gloss, according to Rudolf Bultmann (1971:178).

2. Mishna Nidda 4.1 states: "The daughters of the Samaritans are [deemed unclean as] menstruants from their cradle" (Danby's edition, p. 748). It may reflect an earlier attitude; on this text see Daube 1950:137–47.

3. But see Neyrey 1979:419–37 for Jewish traditions that challenged Jerusalem as the right place of worship; cf. also Coggins 1975:140–42.

4. He "had to (*edei*) go through Samaria" (4:4) suggests either the necessity of taking the shorter way or a divine necessity.

5. Cf. *Pirqe Aboth* 1.5; TalBab *'Erubin* 53b against speaking to women in public (noted by Brown 1966:173).

6. Rudolf Bultmann (1971:78) comments: "Jesus' request for water signified an abandonment of the Jewish viewpoint. The problem is brought out by the astonished question of the woman (v. 9): how can Jesus, as a Jew, ask a Samaritan woman for a drink?" Cf. O'Day 1986:58.

7. Allegorical interpretations of her five husbands — who have been taken to represent various aspects of Samaritan religion — have fallen out of favor.

8. Jacob's well may have provided spring water, because both the terms *pege,* "spring" (4:6, close to "fountain," see LS, s.v. φρέαρ, II) and *phrear,* "well" (4:11, 12, close to "cistern," see LS, s.v. φρέαρ, 2), are used for it here. But this possibility need not destroy the contrast between the "living water" and the water of Jacob's well.

9. For example, see Brown 1966:170. See also n. 14.

10. Some count the sixth hour from 12 o'clock, which would put her trip to the well at a normal time. Against this construal, however, is the fact that nobody besides Jesus seems to be present at the well.

11. Gail R. O'Day warns against assuming the woman had been divorced numerous times, because there are other ways to account for her marital history, e.g., Levirate marriage (Newsom and Ringe 1992:296). In any case, her marital history was irregular and could have drawn criticism or disapproval. Cf. Strack-Billerbeck 2.437.

12. For J. D. M. Derrett (1988:291–98), the living water is water that purifies, and for that reason is needed by the Samaritan woman.

13. Because the woman must have interpreted the living water in the light of Jesus' unexpectedly favorable behavior toward her, it is simplistic to say that she just viewed the living water as magical water and thus totally misunderstood Jesus, as, for example, Josef Blank does: "She had not understood that the point is the new, eschatological existence of human beings, the radical new quality of life which is different from everything earthly" (Blank 1983:9–91), translation mine.

14. Neyrey (1979:422–23) suggests that the tradition of Jacob's well as miraculously overflowing (cf. *Tgs. Yer. I, II; Neof.* Gen 28:10) stands behind the woman's remark: without a bucket, Jesus will have to perform such a miracle to provide water.

15. Jacob played an important role in legitimizing the Samaritans' claim that Gerizim was the right place of worship. See Neyrey 1979:427. Nevertheless, Jewish sources also claim Jacob in support of Jerusalem as the right place of worship. The discussion of the living water of Jesus vs. the water from Jacob's well is a continuation of, not a break with, the Jew-Samaritan issue raised in 4:9, *contra* Bultmann (1971:130–31), who thinks that the issue is not taken up again until verses 20–26.

16. The Samaritans expected a *Taheb*, a prophet like Moses (on the basis of Deut. 18:15–18), not a royal Davidic Messiah, although the term Messiva... is put on the woman's lips in John 4:25. On the Samaritan *Taheb*, see F. Dexinger 1985:27:1–172.

17. On the designation "Savior of the world" as transcending national boundaries, see Koester 1990:665–80.

18. Rensberger (1988:148–49) sees the Johannine community's egalitarianism reflected in the woman's role of bearing witness to Jesus.

19. The historicity of a Samaritan mission by Jesus is debated. Some think that the story in John 4 reflects instead the composition of the Johannine community as including Samaritans.

20. Cf. the association of water with Spirit in the OT (e.g., Ezek. 36:25–27) and Qumran (e.g., 1 QS 4:19–21); cf. also John 3:5, "born of water and the Spirit." The use of the verb *hallesthai* at 4:14 for the "leaping" action of the living water also suggests its identification with the Spirit, which "leaps up" when it falls on a person (e.g., 1 Sam. 10:10 LXX). See Brown 1966:171, 179.

21. Cf. Neyrey 1979:136: "Jesus, who supplants Jacob's well and water, replaces the reality for which well/water are symbols. As 'greater than Jacob' he supplants the old traditions of spirit, cult and knowledge which were associated with Jacob's well."

22. The origin of the universal mission of the Christian church is debated. To what extent is it rooted in Jesus' ministry? The Gospels suggest different answers. For example, the exclusivism of Matthew 10:5–6 (see n. 24) contrasts with the inclusivism of John 4:4–42. But to what degree do texts such as the latter reflect the mission of later Christian communities? (Cf. Scobie 1984:47–60.) It is not my intention to make historical judgments in comparing, on the one hand, the Johannine Jesus' openness to the Samaritan mission and, on the other hand, the Matthean Jesus' reservation about the Gentile mission in the texts discussed.

23. Gerd Theissen (1991:67–68), however, points to evidence for Jewish villages in these parts (Jos *Bell* 2.588; *Vita* 372; *Ap* 1.154), which suggests that Jesus could have found Jews to whom to minister there also. For the socioeconomic background of this pericope I draw further on Theissen in the following discussion.

24. Cf. Matt. 15:24 (see below); also 10:5–6: "Go nowhere among the Gentiles, and enter no town of the Samaritans, but go rather to the lost sheep of the house of Israel."

25. Matthew can be taken to present Jesus' motive as attempting to escape danger. See Gundry 1982:310; Kraft 1981:115.

26. 1 Kings 9:10–14; Jos *Ap* 1.110; *Bell* 3.35; 4.105 with *Ant* 13.154; in the Roman period, *Ant* 18.153.

27. In Mark's version she simply enters a house and falls at his feet and begs.

28. Note the iterative senses of the imperfect *ekrazen*, "kept shouting" (15:22), and the present *krazei*, "keeps shouting" (15:23), followed by the woman's coming and "saying," *legousa* (also present), "Lord, help me!" (15:25).

29. The address *Kyrie* probably means more than the usual "sir," given the woman's belief in Jesus' supernatural powers (Gundry 1993:374).

30. See Michel 1964:1101–2; Strack-Billerbeck 1.724–25, "κύων, κυνάριον."

31. Gundry (1993:373–74), however, challenges the view that in Mark the "children's bread" refers to Jewish evangelism and that the statement should be understood in terms of salvation-history, as in Matthew. Rather, the children are Jesus' disciples, and the bread is the "time and effort needed to teach" them. Whether the children are the Jews or Jesus' Jewish disciples, however, in either case it is Gentiles who are excluded.

32. Not, however, if a faded diminutive (one that has lost its diminutive force). See Gundry 1982:314–15.

33. Cf. Moltmann-Wendel 1986:122: "The result of this activity of women, is that Jesus changes. Thanks to the Canaanite woman Jesus also becomes the helper and healer of the Gentiles"; see also Blank 1983:18. The solution to the difficulty posed by the pericope — namely, that Jesus refuses a request for the healing of a child by saying that "children" are to be preferred to "dogs" — lies in the transformation of Jesus' understanding of his mission through the woman. This growth in understanding of his mission is to be understood in terms of his humanity and does not diminish the fact that Mark and Matthew show a strong interest in portraying Jesus as divine (e.g., Mark 1:11; 2:5–12; 3:11; 9:7; 12:35–37; Matt. 1:23; 2:15; 11:25–27; 14:33; 16:16; 28:19, et al.). Cf. Theissen's critique of three other resolutions of the difficulty of the pericope: the biographical, the paradigmatic, and the salvation-historical interpretations (1991:62–65); cf. also Theissen's own solution: Jesus' rejection of the Gentile woman should be understood in the context of oppression of Jews by Gentiles in the region from which the woman came (:65ff.).

34. In Matt. 8:11–12, Jesus simply notes that at the messianic banquet "many will come from east and west and sit at table with Abraham, Isaac, and Jacob in the kingdom of heaven," whereas "the sons of the kingdom will be thrown into the outer darkness." He then continues his mission to Israel.

35. Further, the Sea of Galilee is associated with Gentiles in 4:13–18.

36. The reader should consult the Greek text for the exact correspondences in terminology of the terms in quotation marks here and in the following sentences.

37. Rudolf Pesch (1980:391) sees a connection between Mark 7:27 (the satisfying of the Jews and then of the Gentiles) and the first and second miraculous feedings, first of the Jews (6:32–44), then of the Gentiles (8:1–9).

2. Exclusion and Embrace

1. This essay was finished in January 1993.

2. For a short analysis of the political and cultural, but mainly philosophical, importance of the "difference," see Taylor 1987:xxi. See also Todorov's (1985) classic treatment of the problem of otherness in the account of the encounter between European and American civilizations.

3. Derrida 1992:10. He says as much when he speaks of the contradictory demand that the European cultural identity not be dispersed but that at the same time it not accept "the capital of a centralizing authority" (:38f.).

4. In his Gifford lectures, Paul Ricoeur distinguishes categorically between *idem-* identity and *ipse-* identity. In the circle of *idem-* identity, the other is "distinct" or "diverse," and it functions as the antonym of "same." In the circle of *ipse-* identity, the otherness is constitutive of sameness; here the selfhood of oneself "implies otherness to such an intimate degree that one cannot be thought of without the other" (Ricoeur 1992:3). So when we speak of the loss of identity — of *Ichlosigkeit* — then the "I" of which the subject says that it is nothing is "a self deprived of the help of sameness" (:166).

5. A stranger, Wiesel (1990:65) writes, "can be of help only as a stranger — lest you are ready to become his caricature. And your own."

6. The metaphor of the door is helpful insofar as it implies a necessary demarcation, but it is also misleading insofar as it suggests a sharp and static boundary. In analyzing the category "Christian," missiologist Paul Hiebert suggests that we make use of the mathematical categories of "bounded sets," "fuzzy sets," and "centered sets." Bounded sets function on the principle "either/or": an apple is either an apple or it is not; it cannot be partly apple and partly a pear. Fuzzy sets, on the other hand, have no sharp boundaries; things are fluid with no stable point of reference and with various degrees of inclusion, as when a mountain merges into the plains. A centered set is defined by a center and the relationship of things to that center, by a *movement* toward it or away from it. The category of "Christian," Hiebert suggests, should be understood as a centered set. A demarcation line exists, but the focus is not on "maintaining the boundary" but "on reaffirming the center" (Hiebert 1983:421–27; see esp. 424). The center of a person who is a new creation in Christ is constituted by separation, but around the center there is space for otherness.

7. "Exclusion" as I am using the term here should not be confused with "separation." Separation, as I noted earlier, is a creative act through which otherness is constituted. If one speaks of sin as separation (see, e.g., Barry Ulanov's [1990:137–50] reflections on sin as separation), one should think of it as a second-order separation — a rendering asunder of things that in their otherness belong together.

8. On the eve of World War II, Carl Gustav Jung (1964:185) wrote: "The impressive thing about the German phenomenon is that one man, who is obviously 'possessed,' has infected a whole nation to such an extent that everything is set in motion and has started rolling on its course towards perdition."

9. Such introjection is possible, of course, because our will to be one with ourselves can be satisfied in part by giving ourselves to others.

10. For the categories, see Kristeva 1988:35ff.

11. This rather schematic analysis of embrace needs to be fleshed out concretely, of course. The identity of a person or social group cannot be abstracted from its history. An embrace must include both individual histories and a common history, which is often a history of pain. The mutual inclusion of histories and of common memory is therefore essential to a genuine embrace.

References Cited

Arendt, Hannah. 1958. *The Human Condition.* Chicago: University of Chicago Press.

Barth, Christoph. 1966. *Introduction to the Psalms.* New York: Charles Scribner's Sons.

Blank, Josef. 1983. Frauen in den Jesus berlieferungen. In *Die Frau im Urchristentum.* Ed. G. Dautzenberg et al. Quaestiones Disputatae 95. Freiburg/Basel/Vienna: Herder.

Block, Robert. 1994. The Tragedy of Rwanda. *The New York Review of Books.* October 20, p. 41.

Brown, Raymond. 1966. *The Gospel According to John I-XII.* Garden City: Doubleday & Co.

Bultmann, Rudolf. 1971. *The Gospel of John: A Commentary.* Trans. G. R. Beasley-Murray. Philadelphia: Westminster Press.

Coggins, R. J. 1975. *Samaritans and Jews: The Origins of Samaritanism Reconsidered.* Atlanta: John Knox Press.

Daube, David. 1950. Jesus and the Samaritan Woman: The Meaning of sugcra'sqai. *Journal of Biblical Literature* 88:69.

Derrett, J. D. M. 1988. The Samaritan Woman's Purity (John 4:4–25). *Evangelical Quarterly* 60:4.

Derrida, Jacques. 1992. *The Other Heading: Reflections on Today's Europe.* Trans. P. A. Brault and M. B. Naas. Bloomington: Indiana University Press.

de Waal, Alex. 1994. The Genocidal State: Hutu Extremism and the Origins of the "Final Solution" in Rwanda. *Times Literary Supplement.* July 1.

Dexinger, F. 1985. Der Taheb: Ein "messianischer" Heilsbringer der Samaritaner. *Kairos* 27.

Feldmeier, Reinhard. 1992. Die Christan als Fremde: Die Metapher der Fremde in der antiken Welt, im Urchristentum und im 1. Petrusbrief. *Wissenschaftliche Untersuchungen zum Neuen Testament* 64. Tübingen: J. C. B. Mohr (Paul Siebeck).

Galen. *De porbis pravissque alimentorum succis.* Cap. 1. Ed Kühn 6.

Gaster, T. H. 1962. Samaritans. *Interpreter's Dictionary of the Bible.* Vol. 4. Nashville/New York: Abingdon Press.

Gerstenberger, Erhard S. 1983. Enemies and Evildoers in the Psalms: A Challenge to Christian Preaching. *Horizons in Biblical Theology* 4:2.

Gibbs, Nancy. 1994. Why? The Killing Fields of Rwanda. *Time.* May 16.

Gundry, Robert H. 1982. *Matthew: A Commentary on His Literary and Theological Art.* Grand Rapids: Eerdmans.

———. 1993. *Mark: A Commentary on His Apology for the Cross.* Grand Rapids: Eerdmans.

Gutiérrez, Gustavo. 1973. *A Theology of Liberation: History, Politics, and Salvation.* Trans. Caridad Inda and John Eagleson. Maryknoll, N.Y.: Orbis Books.

Hampson, Daphne. 1986. Reinhold Niebuhr on Sin: A Critique. In *Reinhold Niebuhr and the Issues of Our Time.* Ed. Richard Harries. Grand Rapids: Eerdmans.

Hiebert, Paul G. 1983. The Category "Christian" in the Mission Task. *International Review of Mission* 72 (July).

Huntington, Samuel P. 1993. The Clash of Civilizations? *Foreign Affairs* 72 (March).

Ignatieff, Michael. 1993. *Blood and Belonging: Journeys into the New Nationalism.* New York: Farrar, Straus & Giroux.

Josephus, Flavius. 1926. *Josephus I: The Life Against Apion.* Vol. 1. Trans. H. St. John Thackeray. Cambridge: Harvard University Press.

Jung, Carl Gustav. 1964. After the Catastrophe: Epilogue to "Essay on Contemporary Events"; and Wotan. In *Collected Works of C. G. Jung.* Ed. Herbert Read et al. Trans. R. F. C. Hull. Bollingen series 20. New York: Pantheon Books.

Kennedy, Paul. 1994. *Preparing for the Twenty-First Century.* New York: Vintage Books.

Koester, Craig R. 1990. "The Savior of the World" (John 4:42). *Journal of Biblical Literature* 109.

Kraft, H. 1981. *Die Entstehung des Christentums.* Darmstadt: Wissenschaftliche Gesellschaft.

Kristeva, Julia. 1988. *Au Commencement était l'amour: Psychoanalyse et foi.* Textes du xxe siècle. Paris: Hachette.

McClendon, James W. 1986. *Systematic Theology I: Ethics.* Nashville: Abingdon Press.

Meecham, Henry G. 1949. *The Epistle to Diognetus 5.5.* In *The Epistle to Diognetus: The Greek Text with Introduction, Translation, and Notes.* Manchester: University of Manchester Press.

Menand, Louis. 1994. The Culture Wars. *The New York Review of Books.* October 20, p. 41.

Michel, O. 1964. *Theological Dictionary of the New Testament* (TDNT). Vol. 3. Grand Rapids: Eerdmans.

Moltmann, Jürgen. 1989. Dient die "pluralistische Theologie" dem Dialog der Welt-religionen? *Evangelische Theologie* 49 (December).

———. 1989. *Der Weg Jesu Christi. Christologie in messianischen Dimensionen.* Munich: Kaiser.

———. 1992. *The Spirit of Life: A Universal Affirmation.* Trans. Margaret Kohl. Minneapolis: Fortress Press.

Moltmann-Wendel, Elisabeth. 1986. *A Land Flowing with Milk and Honey: Perspectives on Feminist Theology.* Trans. John Bowden. New York: Crossroad.

Mouw, Richard J. 1987. Christian Philosophy and Cultural Diversity. *Christian Scholar's Review* 17 (December).

The Multicultural Planet: The Report of a UNESCO International Expert Group. 1993. Ed. Ervin Laszlo. Oxford: Oneworld.

Newsom, Carol A., and Sharon H. Ringe, eds. 1992. John. In *The Woman's Bible Commentary.* Louisville: Westminster/John Knox.

Neyrey, Jerome. 1979. Jacob Traditions and the Interpretation of John 4:10–26. *Catholic Biblical Quarterly* 41.

Niebuhr, Reinhold. 1961. *The Nature and Destiny of Man: A Christian Interpretation I: Human Nature.* New York: Charles Scribner's Sons.

O'Day, Gail. 1986. *Revelation in the Fourth Gospel: Narrative Mode and Theological Claim.* Philadelphia: Fortress Press.

Pannenberg, Wolfhart. 1991. *Systematische Theologie II.* Göttingen: Vandenhoeck & Ruprecht.

Pesch, Rudolf. 1980. *Das Markusevangelium I.* HTKNT. Freiburg/Basel/Vienna: Herder.

Plaskow, Judith. 1980. *Sex, Sin and Grace: Women's Experience and the Theologies of Reinhold Niebuhr and Paul Tillich.* Washington, D.C.: University Press of America.

Rensberger, David. 1988. *Johannine Faith and Liberating Community.* Philadelphia: Westminster Press.

Ricoeur, Paul. 1992. *Oneself as Another.* Trans. K. Blamey. Chicago: University of Chicago Press.

Scobie, C. 1984. Jesus or Paul? The Origin of the Universal Mission of the Christian Church. In *From Jesus to Paul: Studies in Honour of Francis Wright Beare.* Ed. Peter Richardson and John C. Hurd. Waterloo, Ontario: University Press.

Smedes, Lewis B. 1984. *Forgive and Forget: Healing the Hurts We Don't Deserve.* San Francisco: Harper & Row.

Stählin, Gustaf. 1967. xénos ktl. *Theological Dictionary of the New Testament.* Vol. 5. Trans. and ed. Geoffrey W. Bromiley. Grand Rapids: Eerdmans.

Strack, Hermann Leberecht, and Paul Billerbeck. 1922. *Kommentar zum Neuen Testament aus Talmud und Midrasch.* Munich: Beck.

Taylor, Charles. 1992. Politics of Recognition. In *Multiculturalism and Politics of Recognition.* Ed. A. Gutmann. Princeton: Princeton University Press.

Taylor, Mark C. 1987. *Altarity.* Chicago: University Press of Chicago.

Theissen, Gerd. 1991. *The Gospels in Context: Social and Political History in the Synoptic Tradition.* Trans. Linda M. Maloney. Minneapolis: Fortress Press.

Todorov, Tzvetan. 1985. *The Conquest of America: The Question of the Other.* Trans. R. Howard. New York: Harper & Row.

Ulanov, Barry. 1990. The Rages of Sin. *Union Seminary Quarterly Review* 44:1–2.

Volf, Miroslav. Spring 1991. When the Unclean Spirit Leaves: Tasks of the Eastern European Churches After the 1989 Revolution. *Cross Currents* 41:78.

———. 1991. *Work in the Spirit: Toward a Theology of Work.* New York: Oxford University Press.

Wiesel, Elie. 1990. *From the Kingdom of Memory: Reminiscences.* New York: Summit Books.

Wink, Walter. 1992. All Will Be Redeemed. In *The Other Side*.
    November/December.
———. 1992. *Engaging the Powers: Discernment and Resistance in a
    World of Domination*. Minneapolis: Fortress Press.
Wolf, William John. 1956. Reinhold Niebuhr's Doctrine of Man.
    In *Reinhold Niebuhr: His Religious, Social, and Political Thought*.
    Ed. Charles W. Kegley and Robert W. Bretall. New York:
    Macmillan & Co.
Wong, Kun-Chun. 1992. *Interkulturelle Theologie und multikulturelle
    Gemeinde im Matthäusevangelium: Zum Verhältnis von Juden-
    und Heidenchristen im ersten Evangelium*. Freiburg: Universitäts-
    verlag; Göttingen: Vandenhoeck & Ruprecht.
Young, Iris Marion. 1990. *Justice and the Politics of Difference*.
    Princeton: Princeton University Press.